SHIRLEY

from Domesday

to D Day

**Essays by members of the Local History Forum,
edited by John Guilmant and Hilary Kavanagh**

Contributors: Rosaleen Wilkinson, Philippa Newnham, Veronica Green,
John Guilmant, Roy Hawken. AGK Leonard, Reg MacDonald,
Doug Huggins, Glen Curtis, Arne Engesvik, Dave Goddard.

Any profits made from this publication will go towards future projects
covering the people's history of Southampton.

SOUTHAMPTON
CITY COUNCIL

Published by Southampton City Council

Produced by the Community History Unit, City Heritage Services,
Civic Centre, Southampton SO14 7LP.
The Community History Service is provided by City Culture.

CONTENTS

FOREWORD BY COUNCILLOR DORIAN ATTWOOD,
774th Mayor of Southampton

As one who has always been fascinated by Southampton's history, I was delighted to be asked to write the foreword for this book on Shirley.

John Guilmant's knowledge of Shirley is second to none, therefore this book will become the perfect companion for those who take it upon themselves, whether alone or in a group, to walk around this beautiful area of Southampton, and discover, perhaps for the first time, just how important Shirley has been in the development of the city - both now and in the past.

Whilst digging in my own garden I have discovered many relics which I believe originated from the Whitehead Wood estate (Whithedwood). It was this that first fuelled my particular interest in Shirley's history.

In 1990, I was lucky enough to be elected to represent the people of Shirley on the City Council, this led to my meeting a wide range of interesting people whose knowledge of Shirley's past meant that my many questions could be answered, such as "where were German prisoners of war kept in Shirley?", "where was the roller skating rink?" and "where was Shirley's golf course?". These and many more were answered, but they only served to make me hungry for more.

Ancient highways still exist such as Gypsy Grove and Church End, so many stories lay behind Shirley's street names, and of course there's much of interest to be found on the Common.

I know you will enjoy this book and I know it will stimulate debate, as historians often hold differing views.

I commend it to you in the hope that more will follow.

Dorian Attwood

HILL AND UPPER SHIRLEY
Rosaleen Wilkinson

Anyone driving down Hill Lane towards Southampton town centre would see a pleasant residential suburb on one side of the road and a large public Common on the other. Apart from the rather unusual earth banks surrounding the Common there is little visible evidence of the long and interesting history of this district known as Upper Shirley.

The whole area would once have been thickly wooded, sloping gently to the shores of the Test. A stream, Rolles Brook, ran down through the Common and flowed into the estuary about where the Central Station is now. The woods held deer, wild pigs and pigeons, and the unpolluted waters of the Test were full of eels, flat fish and mullet. Altogether it must have been a most attractive area to early settlers and archaeological finds on the Common confirm this. Two flint hand axes dating from 4,000 BC were found by the Cemetery Lake. Two pick-axe type tools made of antlers were also discovered nearby: these dated from about 2,000 BC.

In 1991 an archaeological excavation was carried out on the Bannister Park Bowling and Tennis Club site in Northlands Road, adjacent to the Common. This showed some evidence of prehistoric use. A thin layer of cultivated soil was discovered, well below levels of medieval and modern ploughing, and this suggests prehistoric agricultural activity. Probably crops of rye, wheat and beans would have been grown. These people were Neolithic farmers, living about 2,000 BC. Two flint flakes were found, possibly knives or scrapers, and a substantial number of burnt flints. These may have come from a roasting hearth or have been 'pot boilers': flints heated in a fire, then put into a cooking pot to heat up the contents without standing the pot directly in the flames and risking cracking it. Taken in conjunction with the finds on the Common, the flint axes and antler pickaxes, it seems certain that hunter-gatherers and then Neolithic farming people lived in the area. Perhaps Hill Lane, The Avenue and Winchester Road originated as prehistoric trackways through the woods: many modern roads do have ancient origins.

Certainly Hill Lane is a very ancient route. In the Millbrook Charter of 956 AD a 'hollow way' is mentioned which may be Hill Lane, so even by this early date it was a well established road. In 1992 the excavation of the Hill Farm Unigate Dairy site prior to re-development found evidence to support this. A gravel track was discovered, deeply rutted by cart wheels. This road surface was made by the gradual erosion by traffic and weather down to the naturally occurring gravel layer. A deep lane would have been formed such as is often seen in the countryside where years of cart and animal traffic have worn down the level of the road surface. In Hill Lane a drainage ditch had been dug alongside this roadway.

Not much other archaeological evidence was found. There was a section of medieval flint and limestone cobbling, dated by means of some pottery finds, which may have been a house floor or a paved farm-yard. Near the road there was a circular area of charcoal. It is not certain what this was, but it may have been a lime kiln where limestone was burned to make building mortar. Since bricks were made on the Common this seems a reasonable explanation.

The archaeologists' report concludes that the main medieval activity was further to the south than the area actually excavated. This explains why so little was found of what was really a thriving community. This is rather disappointing but there is plenty of historical evidence available in documentary sources.

In the reign of Edward the Confessor (1042-1066) before the Norman Conquest, a man called Cheping held Shirley for the King. At the time the Domesday Book was written in 1085, Ralph de Mortimer held the manor of Shirley which was in the Buddlesgate Hundred. Shirley manor then consisted of *one hide land for eight ploughs, four villagers and three smallholders with two ploughs, a church, five slaves, a mill worth 30d, a meadow twelve acres, woodland for six pigs, a fishery, and four dwellings in Southampton worth 40d. All valued at 100 shillings.*

The focus of settlement within this manor was probably situated at the junction of Redbridge Hill, Romsey Road and Winchester Road, near the present 'Old Thatched House' Inn, the mill being powered by the confluence of the Hollybrook and Tanners Brook streams. There is no mention of Hill in the Domesday Book but there may well have been a farm there.

Ralph de Mortimer's descendants held the manor until it was acquired by Nicholas of Shirley in 1228. Nicholas is responsible for giving the people of Southampton their Common. In 1228 his right to graze his cattle on the town Common was challenged by the burgesses of Southampton: he claimed the land was part of his manor. Nicholas met the burgesses at Southampton Castle and came to an arrangement. *A fyniall concorde and agreement made between the burgesses of Southampton of thon partie and Nicholas of Sirlie of thother partie for the comon of the same towne in the xiith yeare of the reign of King Henry the sonne of King John.* Under this settlement Nicholas gave up all claim to control of the common pasture of the borough of Southampton, this to remain under the control *of the burgesses and their heirs for ever.* In return he received 10 marks in silver and the promise that the court action against him would be dropped.

The agreement was significant not only because it gave the citizens of Southampton their Common in perpetuity but it also caused the boundaries of the town to be defined more precisely. In 1253 the borough boundaries were described as being *from Achard's bridge* [at the southern end of Hill Lane] *as the road runs, by the crosses to the north as far as Cutthorn* [Bassett Cross-roads] *and from Cutthorn as far as Burleston* [on Burgess Road] *and from Burleston as far as the watercourse at Furzewell* [in South Stoneham] *where it flows into the Itchen.* So Hill and Shirley were outside the town.

In 1233 Nicholas of Shirley gave gifts of timber from his lands towards the construction of a Franciscan Friary in Southampton. Then in 1240 he

granted revenue from Shirley Church, which until then had belonged to his manor, to St Denys priory. Other members of his family were also benefactors of St Denys.

In 1272 Nicholas, the grandson of Nicholas of Shirley, granted the mill and land in Shirley to Nicholas de Barbeflete. *Nicholas de Shyrle granteth unto Nicholas de Barflet and Alice his wife and ther heyrs all his tenement land and rents in Schirley with a myll.* The Barbefletes were a wealthy family who had earned their money from trading in wool and wine in Southampton. It often happened that families who had been successful in commerce sought to improve their social status by buying land. In 1290 Nicholas de Barbeflete granted the use of the spring of Colewell at Hill (presently in the grounds of Nazareth House) to the Franciscan Friars. Work began in 1304 on a water conduit which took fresh water via the waterhouse (in Commercial Road) right down to the Friary inside the walled town.

Sadly, these rich families suffered from the high infant mortality prevalent at the time and often lost their direct heirs. This happened to the Barbefletes. Nicholas de Barbeflete died in 1294 leaving a son and heir, also Nicholas, who was a minor. He died in 1311. The manor then passed to his cousin Richard de Barbeflete who in fact seems to have been administering the manor's affairs for several years already.

In 1308 Richard de Barbeflete bought land from the Prior and Convent of St Swithun, Winchester, who were lords of the manor of Millbrook. Richard obviously intended to improve and extend the mill at Shirley because the agreement was made with the proviso that if he made a mill-pond it must not hinder the tenants of the manor of Millbrook from getting to their adjoining land. Richard was an important burgess in Southampton and was mayor in 1317, but in 1328 he was dismissed from the office of tronage of wool, *he does not behave himself well in the said office,* and after this the family fortunes declined.

In 1329 Richard de Barbeflete died without any surviving children and the manor was inherited by his widow, Matilda of Holbury. In 1333 Matilda settled the manor on Sir Roger Norman and his wife Joan. He might have been a distant relative but it is more likely that it was simply sold to him. In his generation Sir Roger Norman held the widest extent of rural properties ever owned by a Southampton burgess. He owned land in Millbrook, Shirley, Hill and Chilworth, and estates in Wiltshire, Gloucestershire, Essex and Suffolk.

Sir Roger Norman was mayor of Southampton from 1328-31 and was probably the richest burgess of his day. He had made his money trading on a large scale in wool. He lived in the parish of Holy Rood in Southampton and although he did not live in Hill he did concern himself personally with affairs there. In July 1347 he witnessed a charter concerning lands belonging to William Ace in Hill.

Sir Roger was a friend and business associate of John le Fleming, who lived in the manor house at Shirley. An interesting incident involving John is recorded in contemporary documents. John was a wealthy burgess who seems to have been rather unpopular. In 1327 Henry, Walter and John Forst accused him of fraudulently obtaining money belonging to the town. They got together a group of rowdies and burned John's property in Southampton, and then marched out to Shirley where they attacked the manor house and imprisoned him until he paid up £72 acquittance on a debt. This attack may have been due to personal jealousy between the Flemings and the Forsts, or it could be an indication of rising popular antagonism towards rich landowners and their comparatively luxurious lifestyle. It reflects a general atmosphere of lawlessness in England around this time. Nothing more is recorded about this incident.

During the years that Sir Roger Norman was lord of the manor of Shirley and Hill, several disasters befell Southampton. The first of these was the French raid and sacking of the town on 4 October 1338. Although the attack did not directly involve the inhabitants of Hill they must have seen the fires as the town burned and perhaps gave assistance to victims who fled into the countryside. Markets and trade were ruined as a result of the raid.

Then the weather that winter of 1338 was particularly severe. A chronicler records that *from the beginning of October to the beginning of the month of December there fell such rains that the ground was rendered quite saturated and due to this there was no sowing. And in the beginning of the month of December came a very hard frost so that the whole of the saturated ground was completely frozen and the whole earth was seen to be like ice. This frost lasted twelve weeks whence the whole of the winter sowing was as if dead so that in March, April and May almost nothing appeared.* It is easy to imagine their discomfort, wet and cold, in their miserable little houses at the bottom of Hill Lane, and the hunger and hardship which resulted from the failed harvests.

Ten years after the French raid, Southampton had still not recovered from the damage and loss of trade, and then came the Black Death. Some chroniclers at the time said that the disease-carrying rats entered England from Europe via the port of Southampton, although later opinion suggests it was through Melcombe Regis in Dorset. In the warmer weather of spring 1349 the plague-bearing fleas multiplied rapidly and the disease spread. There was certainly high mortality in the town and although there are no recorded figures for outlying villages, Hill and Shirley cannot have escaped. The Black Death struck hardest at the weakest sections of the population, the old and the young. In the first wave of the plague about a third of the population died, but a second outbreak in 1361 took still more, especially children. In the two outbreaks overall, half the population died. The deaths of so many children meant that there were few young adults to have families in later years, so the birth rate declined disastrously. Population numbers did not recover until the early 1500s. It may be significant that there is no mention of Hill or Shirley in historical records from the time of the Black Death in 1349 until the mid 1400s.

When Sir Roger Norman died in 1347 he left his property to his grandson Giles Norman who was a minor. The custody of the manor was entrusted to John Inkpen whilst Giles was still a child, but sadly the boy died in 1362 before he came of age. He may have been a victim of the second outbreak of the Black Death affecting England in 1361-2, which particularly struck at children. Giles' heir was his cousin Margaret, wife of John Chamberlayne, and then the property went to their daughter Alice who married a Richard Becket. So in 1391 Alice and Richard Becket were lords of the manor of Shirley and Hill. There were no sons in the family and the manor passed on the female line to Joan, wife of Robert Peny and she sold it to Robert Whitehead in 1433.

In the years since the Black Death it would seem that the mill at Shirley, which Richard de Barbeflete had rebuilt, or extended and improved, in 1308, had been deserted. It had fallen into disrepair and the stream and sluices had silted up. In 1433 Robert Whitehead, the new lord of the manor, made an agreement with the prior and convent of St Swithun who were lords of the manor of Millbrook. *That where of old a myll hath been sett at Sherley att a place called Sherley Bridge, the hed whereof was as well upon ther mannor of Milbroke as the landes of Robert Whithed, part of his mannor of Hull, they now grant all ther parte of the scite of the said myll, there to bee new builte with libertye to make scluses.*

The re-built mill in Shirley was rented out by John Whitehead, Robert's son, to a miller called Robert Orchard in 1465 at 3s 4d per annum for a term of thirty years, along with two ponds, fishing and fowling. However, Robert Orchard only stayed for part of his term, and the mill was re-let to John Springe in 1478 at the higher rent of 6s 8d annually, for a period of twenty years. John Springe was obviously an enterprising man because he also ran a batryware business in Southampton. Batryware was copper or pewter kitchen utensils and pans.

History tends to deal with the lives of Kings and Queens, or at least the rich and powerful, and there is little evidence about how the poor and ordinary residents of the manor lived. Most of the inhabitants of Shirley and Hill would have been employed by the tenant farmer as labourers growing crops for home consumption and for sale in the markets of Southampton. Hours of work lasted as long as the hours of daylight and only attendance at church on Sundays or the religious festivals at Christmas, Easter and All Saints (1 November) gave much respite.

However there is also evidence to show that artisans and craftsmen unconnected with agriculture worked in Hill. One of these was a carpenter called Robert Orchard. He was probably the same man who had been the miller at Shirley. In 1474 it is recorded that Robert Orchard at Hill

supplied the wood for a new Scold's Throne at West Hall in Southampton. This was for punishing those *who would not please to moderate the rancour of their tongues.*

Another artisan was John Bowner of Hill. During 1478 the Brokage Book (account books which recorded the tax paid on all goods taken out through the Bargate) records deliveries of materials used in dyeing; madder, alum and wood. Judging by the quantities he was working on a fairly small scale, but was successful enough to afford a servant to run his errands. These records are interesting because they suggest that Hill was not just a farmstead, but a community containing crafts and small-scale industry.

The manor prospered under the lordship of the Whiteheads. The Southampton Brokage Books show that many consignments of luxury goods, such as French wine, figs, raisins and almonds, were sent by cart to the manor houses at Shirley and Hill from the town in the latter half of the fifteenth century.

By the late 1400s larger farmsteads had developed into courtyards with buildings for living quarters separate from the cattle byres. Houses themselves had been much improved by the introduction of brick-built fireplaces and chimneys around the same period. Previously the English home had consisted of a single long room, shared by livestock in the winter, with a central hearth and a hole in the roof to let the smoke out.

The Whitehead family, who lived at Norman's Court at Tytherley, had been lords of the manor of Shirley and Hill since 1433. (Norman's Court is still in existence as a preparatory school, Northaw School at East Tytherley, and there is still a large Norman's Court Estate in the area.) It is from them that Whitehead's Wood and modern Whithedwood Avenue take their names. Whitehead's Wood stretched from the upper part of Hill Lane down towards Shirley. One of the long line of Whiteheads, Augustine, died in 1557, leaving the manor to his wife Julian for life, to revert on her death to his son and heir Richard, who was still a minor. Julian re-married in 1569, and she and her new husband leased the manor house and its land at Hill to Thomas Fashyn, gentleman, for twenty-one years.

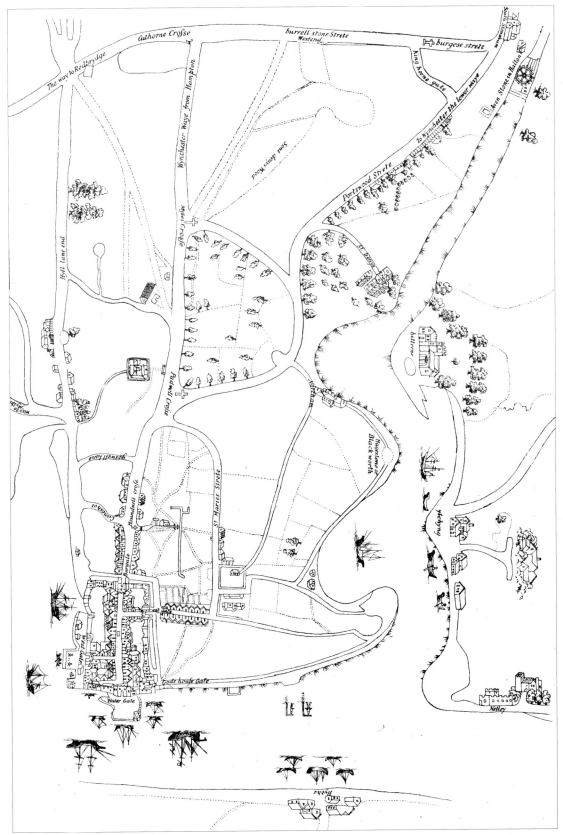

The way to Redbryge

Guthorne Crofse

burrell stone Strete Westend

burgese strete

King horne gate

Wynchester Waye from Hampton

to Wynchester the lower waye

Aven Stone in Hulton

Portswood Strete

St Denis Wood

St Deny

butterne

Hyll lane end

Padwell Crofse

Hauestone or Black worth

goswell farm

to Romsey

Houndwell crofse

Hitchyng

St Maries Strete

Barre gate

Gods house Gate

Water Gate

Netley

Hitham

Original Southampton University

Line-drawn copy. 'Southampton Atlas' WH Rogers 1907.
This early map, popularly known as the 'Elizabethan' map, is thought to have been drawn by a person with local knowledge at some time between 1550 and 1650. The original is painted. Unfortunately it was extensively overpainted in the early nineteenth century, so details cannot be relied upon. However the substantial courtyard farmstead which is depicted at Hill would be in keeping with the period.

5

Thomas Fashyn emerges from the obscurity and anonymity of the past as an interesting, contentious personality, losing his home and money, and, with his family, declining into decadence. He was quite a wealthy man. His father had been a merchant and mayor of Southampton and had died in 1558 bequeathing to Thomas a number of houses in Southampton and a house called Freemantel in the parish of Millbrook. Thomas married Alice Wythoc in 1558 and on 16 August 1569 they moved into the manor house at Hill. It must have been a substantial and comfortable house to be worthy of a rich man. He then proceeded to be a thorn in the side of the burgesses of Southampton by grazing his cattle on the Common. In 1569 he was in trouble at the Court Leet for overstocking the common with sixty sheep. Then on 17 July 1571 *Hugh Emery and John Manfyide and other dryvers of the Comyne of the towne of Suthampton found nigh unto the brick kyln uppon the grene theare, nyne hoggs of the goods and chattells of Thomas Fashin, dwelling in the manor howyse of Hyll. And from thence dyd dryve them and impound them and the said Thomas was adjudged to paye for the same trespass 4d.*

Thomas may well have encouraged another tenant farmer at Hill, William Springe, to challenge the grazing regulations. William was probably a descendant of the John Springe who had rented Shirley Mill in 1478. On 24 July 1571 William Springe *one of the tenants of the lord of Hill hath compounded and paid to the mayor and burgesses 12d for the trespass of five kine [cows] of his upon the heath called the Common.* Anyway, the burgesses would have none of it and the Remembrance Book records *it is concluded and agreed by Mr Mayor and his brethren that where there is controversy between Richard Whitehead, gentleman, who as lord of the manor was ultimately responsible and the burgesses, touching the right of the Common, belonging to the town of Southampton, that the trial thereof shall be tried by order of law.* The town claimed that while the east side of Hill Lane lay within the boundaries of Southampton, Hill itself, which was on the west side, did not and could not claim rights in the adjoining Common.

The outcome of the trial is not recorded but it may be significant that in September 1576 Richard Whitehead, now of age, bought back the remaining fourteen years of the lease on Hill farm from his troublesome tenant for £120. After Thomas Fashyn left the manor house at Hill, or was perhaps turned out of the house, he went to live in St Michael's parish in Southampton. By 1599 he was no longer a wealthy gentleman, his property being valued at only £15. His sons also abandoned respectable behaviour. On 25 September 1608 Walter Fashyn, his second son, was accused, along with Alice his maid and three other women, of stealing bedding from Peter Herevill. Two years later his other son Henry was charged with being a common haunter of ale-houses and *there to live disorderly and dishonestly.* No more is heard of the Fashyns, but it is interesting to speculate on the causes of the family's decline.

Altogether the residents of Hill seem to have been a nuisance to the burgesses of Southampton and numerous complaints about them appear in Court Leet records. For example, in 1569: *Wateridge and Millet sent 60 sheep to graze on the Common from Hyll. Fined 2s 6d each.* In 1574 *Wateridge of Hill fined for digging two cart loads of clay from the saltmarsh which was for Mr Cartmell. Fined 20s.* In 1575 *The highway going to Hill is greatly decayed in places, if speedy redress thereof be not made the carts will not be able to pass that way in winter. There is a very noisome dunghill made by them of Hill upon the highway to Hill. Be it commanded to them that hath layed the same there to carry it away upon pain of 20s.* In 1582 *Refuse near the cattle watering places near the bottom of Hill Lane to be cleared away.* Finally, in 1587 *Nicholas Roch having made a dock for the having out of his ship that was driven by foul weather upon the shore and highway towards Hill, has left the same unfilled which is dangerous for any that by right may pass that way.*

It was during the last part of the sixteenth century that the old church at Shirley disappeared. A church is mentioned at Shirley in Domesday Book in 1085, but in 1574 Shirley parish was amalgamated with Millbrook parish, and the church was probably not used much after this date. *1st May 1574. Robert Lanson and William Reade, wardens of Shirley church and Radulph Matthias and William Mansbrigg wardens of Millbrook church being present. The parish church of Shirley was in existence in far removed time as it now exists, rather small and in straitened circumstances. All tithes and rents pertaining to it do not exceed £5. The church of*

Shirley is becoming in a state of ruin. All the parishioners of Shirley can easily hear divine service in Millbrook. The church of Millbrook is sufficiently proper, furnished and large enough to hold all the parishioners of Millbrook and Shirley. We annexe to the possession of Richard Byrde, incumbent of Millbrook for all future time. We subject the parish church of Shirley with its cemetery to the said Millbrook church as to a mother church.

The church was finally pulled down in 1609 and stones from it were used to enlarge St Nicholas' church at Millbrook. It seems appropriate at this point to jump forward two centuries and complete the story. In the 1860s workmen digging sand and gravel found over two hundred skeletons on the lower declivity [slope] of the hill leading from old to new Shirley. Artefacts probably associated with a church were found, including a brass cross and a bell, but unfortunately none of this evidence was carefully excavated and documented. It would seem that the church and burial ground was somewhere in the middle of the road junction of Winchester Road, Redbridge Hill, Romsey Road and the modern Tebourba Way, on the level area just before the road rises up to new Shirley and towards Romsey the other way.

The early years of the seventeenth century were characterised by an enthusiasm for rules and regulations governing trades and markets and employment, and several residents of Hill fell foul of these. The Southampton Assembly Book 10 March 1608 records a complaint by John Dale and other glove makers about a newcomer glover dwelling at Hill. He sold his gloves openly in the market in Southampton, but it was ruled that as he lived outside the town he could not be controlled and made to sell his gloves in a shop. In 1618 Thomas Cawle, a felt maker from Hill was fined for *casting out his washing water and soapie suds wherewith he usually washeth his hats and such like at Hill bridge.* It throws an interesting light on life in Hill and its occupations.

The Whitehead family were lords of the manor from 1433 to 1777, and were influential people in the town. In 1602 Sir Henry Whitehead was a Justice of the Peace and Sheriff of Southampton and as such closely involved in local government. Idle, wanton behaviour was strongly disapproved of,

probably because rate payers did not want to spend money supporting the undeserving poor. A letter from Sir Henry Whitehead's letter book 21 March 1602 illustrates his strict attitude very well. *It is agreed that a general watch and search shall be made in every town and village in this country upon Saturday next and that a diligent and privie search shall be made in all inns, alehouses and other suspected places for all rogues, vagabonds and other idle, dissolute and masterless persons of strong and able bodies, and such as be so shall be taken unto the Justice of the Peace.*

The Poor Laws concerned themselves with pauper children and there is a sad little story involving Hill. 26 June 1612: *this day Robert Goosey aged five years, a poor child born in this town son of Thomas Goosey, lately deceased, and having no friends or means to relieve or maintain him, was put apprentice to Nicholas Lovelocke and his wife Christian of Hill, husbandman, for sixteen years. They are to keep him and bring him up in husbandry* [farming]. *His sister Amy, aged four years to be put with William Beckley in Southampton, serge weaver, as apprentice, to find meat, drink and lodging and apparel and other things convenient for her. His sister Francis aged ten years to be put apprentice to John Young, viteler, to age twenty-one.* It is not clear whether these children reached adulthood and eventually had families of their own, or whether they succumbed to hardship or neglect or one of the many ills threatening children then.

Throughout the 1600s epidemics of plague broke out from time to time, culminating in the Great Plague of 1665. It has been estimated that there were at least 1,700 plague victims in Southampton during the seventeenth century out of a population which seldom rose above 4,000. There was a bad outbreak in 1604 when church registers recorded hundreds of people as *died of the plague.* Unfortunately the surviving register of Millbrook Parish Church does not begin until 1633 so there are no records of the deaths that must have occurred in Hill and Shirley in that outbreak.

The combined effects of plague and the loss of trade in wine and wool had caused a decline in the general prosperity of Southampton since the Middle Ages. So the visits of Charles I in 1627 and 1635 were not very welcome because of the expenses in which they involved the town, especially the billeting of troops and the forced loans that had to be made to the King. This resentment probably lay behind the majority of the townsfolk supporting the Parliamentary side during the civil war which broke out in 1642. It is to be hoped that the villagers of Hill sympathised with that view because their lord of the Manor, Sir Richard Whitehead (Sir Henry, his father, had died in 1629) was a prominent Roundhead.

Southampton was garrisoned with Parliamentary troops in December 1642. In 1643 the town was threatened when the Royalist Colonel Hopton took Romsey and even broke down the bridge at Redbridge. It must have been an anxious time for the people of Millbrook and Shirley with war practically on their doorsteps. However, Colonel Richard Norton led Parliamentary troops against Romsey and the Royalists were routed. The Royalists retreated west after the battle of Cheriton in March 1644, and Colonel Sir Richard Whitehead, earlier involved in the siege of Basing House, was left to besiege Bishops Waltham Palace. He had instructions to pull it down if he so desired. Unfortunately he did.

No documents are available recording details of the life of Hill or Shirley during the Puritan era or the Restoration of the monarchy, but in 1662 the Hearth Tax was imposed to help alleviate Charles II's financial difficulties. Every household had to be registered and interesting facts about the village of Hill are revealed. The tax charged 2s annually on every hearth or stove within all dwellings, payable in equal instalments on Lady Day and Michaelmas. Those who owned goods worth less than £10 or lived in a house costing less than £1 a year rent were exempt. Less than three hearths denotes a degree of poverty, more than ten suggests considerable affluence. Every house in Hill was registered. There were thirty six households so it was really quite a large village. It had been thought that until Victorian times when many villas were built along Hill Lane, Hill was simply a large estate. This register proves conclusively that it was still a substantial community, just as records from previous centuries had suggested.

Mr Edmund Exton was the gentleman at the manor house, he had eleven hearths. John Dorneford and

William Evans with seven each were well off. Two households had five and one had four hearths, but the majority of homes in the village were obviously poor, nineteen being below the poverty mark of two or fewer hearths. A further six households were exempt entirely, being so poor they did not even own £10 worth of goods.

The particular interest of this document is that it enables the identification of residents of Hill who died in the Great Plague of 1665. The plague, it is said, was brought to Southampton by a child who was smuggled out of London, no doubt in the hope of saving him, and landed at Millbrook shore by boat. The contagion rapidly spread in the town until the mayor was left with only one magistrate and a handful of the assembly to carry on local government. In Hill, five people died during the Plague period, Andrew Jones, Thomas Starke, Eales, daughter of William Goater, and William Wheeler and his wife, who were *buried in their own grounds, being suspected to die of Plague*. The severe measures of imprisoning sufferers in their homes, still in force at this time, seems to have been fairly effective in confining the Plague in Hill. All the victims lived in the poorest houses.

Elsie Sandell, the local historian, believed that during the Great Plague of 1665, the shops and market in Southampton were closed and trade was at a standstill. A market was set up at Four Posts and people from the countryside nearby, for example Hill, Shirley and Millbrook, supplied food for the townsfolk. Business was transacted across the stream at a safe distance. Goods were hoisted over the Rolles Brook near Achard's bridge and the money to pay for the purchases was placed in a receptacle which was immersed in the stream to guard against infection.

As the seventeenth century drew to a close Southampton took on the character of a modern community as distinct from a medieval one and Hill was gradually drawn more into the life of the town, away from its origins as a country manor. The nature of the manor itself too was changing. After the death of the Roundhead Sir Richard Whitehead the manor was held by his son Francis. Francis' son Henry married a Mary Norton and for the first time since 1433 no male heir was born so the manor passed to their daughter Mary in 1717. She married Alexander Thistlethwayte and so the long Whitehead line ended. From this time onwards, the land of the manor was progressively sold off, much of it to the Atherley family. Arthur Atherley was twice mayor of Southampton in 1707 and 1717. He was the founder of the fortunes of the family. He had been apprenticed to an ironmonger but became a prosperous merchant and the Atherleys went on to become local landowners and bankers. Generations of Atherleys were active in local affairs, several being mayor, and by 1830 they owned almost all the land on the west side of Hill Lane. The Reverend Arthur Atherley, born in 1794, provided funds for elm trees to be planted along Hill Lane in 1848. These died of Dutch elm disease in recent years.

In the eighteenth century Southampton developed as a spa town. From about 1730 the town began to be a popular resort, the climate was considered mild but bracing and wealthy gentry not only came to drink the waters but to build fine residences such as Bellevue, Banister Court, Freemantle House, Springhill House and a host of smaller select villas. In 1759 Frederick, Prince of Wales visited the town and Southampton's status as a fashionable place was confirmed. The Southampton Guide of 1791 reported that *The inhabitants of Southampton and its environs enjoy the most pure and salubrious atmosphere. There are few chronic disorders where bathing in the salt water may not be serviceable and drinking it medicinally has frequently been attended with the happiest results.*

Elegant society balls and concerts were held at the Polygon and the Duke of Cumberland, George III's brother, often stayed in the town to enjoy 'the season' until about 1778. During the 1770s the New Road (now Commercial Road) was constructed from the end of Above Bar Street through the West Marlands to the shore near Four Posts. This replaced the old route to Hill, Redbridge and beyond, along Canshut or Windmill Lane, which had followed the shoreline. The name Four Posts is said to have been given to the area around the bottom of Hill Lane because the old medieval road from the town crossed Rolles brook at Achard's bridge (also known as Hill Bridge and Acorn Bridge) and four names or direction posts were erected to point out the ways from the

junction: the roads to Romsey and Shirley, Millbrook and Redbridge, to Southampton and north to Hill.

A little group of cottages grew up along the road by Four Posts, and also down the hill towards the shoreline: this part was known as Sidford. The walk from the town out to Four Posts where there was a public house *much frequented upon excursions* was considered very charming.

From 1793 the Revolutionary and Napoleonic wars led to conflict between England and France for twenty-two years. Indeed one member of the French aristocracy sought refuge in Hill. In the Millbrook Parish register it is recorded that *Rene Hyacinth Philip de Huquet, Knight and Patron of Hauteville, Normandy, died at Hill 27th September 1794.*

The French wars did have one advantage in that they brought the military into town, making Southampton very crowded and gay. In 1795 troops bound for the West Indies were camped on Shirley Common. In 1799 six regiments of foot who were to form part of an expedition to Holland were encamped on Shirley Common before their departure. Their ensuing success in capturing the Dutch fleet was greatly celebrated in the town. The campsite is shown on a map of 1802 as being near the top of Hill Lane. The camp was used again in 1803 for the training of local militia. All men between seventeen and fifty were liable to be called and had twenty-eight days training each year. A review of two thousand local volunteers of the Loyal Southampton, Millbrook, Stoneham and Romsey Corps was held by the Duke of Cumberland, one of the younger sons of George III, on Shirley Common in December 1803. Local tradition claims that the massive Monterey pine tree just inside the Bellemoor Gate of the Southampton Common was planted by the Duke to commemorate this occasion. The truth of this cannot be established but judging by its size it seems possible.

In the last quarter of the eighteenth century, apart from the buildings around Hill, there were no other houses in Hill Lane, as is shown on a map of 1778. By 1791 Cockerwood House appears; this was variously known as Cockroach Farm or

Cockroads Farm. The house, much modernised, is still in existence next to the caretakers' lodge of Taunton's College (previously the Girls' Grammar School). Despite the elegance and sophistication of Southampton, not far outside town the countryside was very sparsely populated and still rather wild and dangerous. The Hampshire Chronicle reports that *on Monday October 25th 1784 as his worshipful the Mayor of this town and his daughter were returning home in a single horse chaise they were stopped, about four o'clock in the afternoon, near the Cowherds, by a single highwayman, who robbed them of their watches and money. The man was shabbily dressed in a light coloured coat and red waistcoat and rode a very bad horse.*

This isolation was soon to end however. The Thistlethwaytes, successors to the Whitehead lords of the manor, sold their land to Gifford Warriner. He was unfortunately declared a lunatic in 1821. His trustees came together with the Atherley Family to promote an act of parliament for the enclosure of *Shirley Common sometimes also called Hill or Whitehead's Wood Common, containing by estimation four hundred acres or thereabouts.* This act was passed 22 May 1829. The land surveyor was John Hayward who held meetings at the Star Inn. J D Doswell laid out boundaries, ten public carriageways, two bridleways and three footways. The unusual street plans in several places can be traced to original field boundaries.

Rosaleen Wilkinson
Bellemoor Road was once an un-named track alongside a field boundary. It took its name from Bellemoor House which was owned by the Reverend James Crabb who lived at Springhill Court. Bellemoor House was on the site of 'The Mews' and was demolished in the 1970s.

In 1830, the land was allotted to individual ownership, roads were laid out and after this, residential development proceeded steadily under the pressure of the expanding population of Southampton. A map produced for the enclosure shows several private houses between Hill Farm and Four Posts. There was also the mansion of Springhill Court, and then, further north up Hill Lane, Cockroads Farm. Just beyond what is now Bellemoor Road there were several single storey cottages within small-holdings. These were owned by Mr Wright, Mr Young, Mr Curtis, Mr Wills, Mr Kingswell, Mr Ellyet and Mrs Ralfe.

Rosaleen Wilkinson
One of the cottages in Upper Hill Lane shown on the 1830 map.

Shirley Common was gradually brought under cultivation by market gardeners supplying the expanding Shirley Village and big houses like Hollybrook, Malvern House and Whithedwood House, which were being built around the 1830s. The hamlet around Bellemoor Road was known as Upper Hill and was described in the 'Stranger's Guide' 1856 as *lying scattered at the side of Hill Lane, marked by overhanging trees and graced with pretty cottages and villas with flower and market gardens in the highest state of cultivation.* In 1855 a Mr B Webb set up as a beer retailer in the two front rooms of a cottage which stood roughly on the site of the present Hill Lane petrol station. This inn was called 'The Good Intent' and was apparently popular with Southampton people taking walks to the Common and Hill Lane. 'Rural Walks' 1870 describes the area. *It furnishes delightful walks in connection with the Shirley and Southampton footpaths although it is dusty in summer and dirty after much rain.* The successor to

'The Good Intent' was established in the early 1900s on the site of Bellemoor Cottage and became the Bellemoor Inn.

After Mr Webb the publican died in 1865 his widow ran a large market garden which stretched from Hill Lane down to Edwards' Nurseries (now the grounds of Bellemoor Boys' School). Mrs Webb's nursery was noted for its flowers and people came from the villages of Shirley and Highfield to buy them. In addition to a pony for her trap, Mrs Webb also kept pigs and goats which she and her labourers were permitted to graze on the Common for an annual fee of 2s. She was also permitted to make a small opening in the earthen banks of the Common to let her animals through. This little gateway was to be seen opposite 286 Hill Lane until 1994 when it was blocked off again, but the dropped kerb still shows where it was. In 1881 Mrs Webb had a terrace of cottages built for her labourers, Perseverance Cottages, and had one added at the end for herself four years later. The original bill for the construction of the cottages shows that the first three cost £333 0s 0d, digging of wells £2 0s 0d, papering three cottages £3 2s 1d, one thousand bricks cost £1 9s 0d, and paint and iron bars £1 14s 0d.

Another resident of Upper Hill in Victorian times was Granny Bone who was a washerwoman. Her little brick built wash-house with its chimney still stood and was used as a store on the forecourt of the garage until modernisation in the 1970s.

Once Shirley Common was enclosed and sold off in lots in the 1830s land became available for the building of country houses. The Hampshire Advertiser on 8 August 1836 remarks that *we are glad to observe the progress of the works, private and public, on Shirley Common. Villas are fast rising there, creating the appearance of a populous and genteel occupation of what is well known to be one of the most beautiful and healthy spots in our picturesque neighbourhood. The road is now completed from Hill Lane through the Warriners' estate connecting the* [Shirley] *Common very readily with our town.*' The population of Shirley was expanding rapidly in the 1830s and the old parish church of Millbrook served 2,375 inhabitants in 1836, and was obviously much too small. Land for a new church was given by Nathaniel Jefferys of Hollybrook

House, and money for the building came from the Church Building Society and from the personal funds of Reverend William Orger from Sydenham in Kent. He gave £2,800 towards the construction of the church and a house for the incumbent. The first vicarage was in Winchester Road opposite the end of Wordsworth Road and later was incorporated into the Children's Hospital.

St James' Church was consecrated on 20 August 1836, an event which was reported in the Hampshire Advertiser. *The new church of St James, Shirley, was consecrated this morning by the Bishop of Winchester. A crowded congregation attended to witness the ceremony, notwithstanding the unfavourable weather. On the entry of the Bishop of Winchester at the door of the church, a suitable voluntary was most delightfully played by Mr Truss the organist. The petition for consecration was presented by Mr W. Orger. It contains six hundred sittings. At the back of the altar is a gothic screen, divided into three components, the outer entablatures contain the Commandments, the Lord's Prayer and the Belief, the centre entablature the crucifixion by Shayer, a first rate painting, the head of life itself and the expression of subdued anguish is beautifully conceived and awakes the feeling of an intense degree of interest. It is one of the happiest of his late products.* [This picture has disappeared]. *After the service the Lord Bishop and a select party partook of refreshments at the residence of the incumbent.*

Mr Orger, the first vicar of Shirley, wore a top hat, tail coat, breeches and high boots and had luxuriant side whiskers. He rode around the quiet lanes of Shirley on a grey mare. The church was considered to be in the country and in winter Evensong was held in the early afternoon. Sunday morning services lasted until 1 pm and Mr Orger's sermons were at least an hour long. However, he was very popular and there was a huge crowd, mostly of poor people, at his funeral.

Only four years after its consecration the capacity of the church had to be increased to over a thousand by the installation of balconies in 1840. In 1881 new pews and a new chancel were added. The church clock was provided by public subscription in 1875. In 1994 the church underwent radical internal alterations with the removal of the pews, the levelling of the floor and redecoration. The

St James' Church in about 1926

floor was carpeted and the pews replaced by modern chairs.

One resident of Hill in the 1830s was Captain Rainier, a retired naval officer and a member of the Corporation of Southampton. He played a significant part in averting local conflict when in 1830 a wave of agricultural labourers' riots broke out in Kent and spread along the South Coast. The riots were provoked by low wages, and a hatred of new technology in the form of threshing machines which were blamed for throwing men out of work. Added to the labourers' dissatisfaction were the harsh and degrading methods of poor relief. In late November Southampton was thrown into a state of excitement by reports of violence and gatherings of farm labourers in the neighbourhood. Threatening letters were received by local landowners from 'Captain Swing' - hence the name Swing Riots given to these disturbances: the ring leaders said that they 'would swing' (i.e. be hanged) before they gave up their demands. On 28 November labourers gathered at Shirley to demand an increase in wages. Riots and machine

breaking had occurred at Fair Oak the previous day so law-abiding people were rather frightened. Captain Rainier swore in a hundred Special Constables to preserve the peace. In the evening he met with local farmers and landowners and they agreed to pay their men 12s a week during the winter. This action avoided the *vast assemblages*, machine breaking and violent behaviour which took place in villages around.

The substantial community of thirty-five cottages which constituted Hill in the mid 1600s had disappeared by the middle of the nineteenth century. On a map of 1866 Hill Farm is still evident but next to it is an extensive orchard called Hill Garden where the original village must have been. There were several villas at the southern end of Hill Lane; Lawn Cottage, Park Cottage, Laurel Cottage, Park House, Clifton Place and York Lodge. Hill had now become a genteel residential area, popular with retired officers and professional gentlemen.

A charming description of Hill and Sidford in the last years of the nineteenth century was printed in the

Hampshire Advertiser in 1935. *The Commercial Road end of Hill Lane is narrow and in summer almost arched over by the boughs of trees. Some of the old cottages of Sidford still stand in the narrow hidden away terraces around the central station. There are no fishermen hauling shiny wet nets up Nelsons' Hill these days, but in the rural gardens of Sidford hollyhocks still bloom and sweet peas clamber over fences.*

City Heritage Collections
Four Posts Mission Room, which was located on the north side of Millbrook Road, between Shirley Road and Osbourne (now Bourne) Road.

HILL FARM

In 1823 Alfred Brown took over Hill Farm and made it into a dairy farm supplying milk to the surrounding homes. In addition to dairy cows and cart horses there were pigs, goats and poultry on the farm. Housing development had gradually surrounded the farm by 1907 but it remained as a working, productive dairy right until the Second World War.

In 1940, as part of Government food production plans, Brown's Hill Farm dairy merged with Harrisons' Shirley based dairy to become Brown and Harrisons'. After the war the land around the farm was given over to allotments and the main farm buildings were used as offices and a depot for milk deliveries; it was no longer a productive dairy. The horses used to pull milk carts were stabled at Stratton Road in Shirley: at one time there were three hundred horses. In 1957 Brown and Harrisons' became South Coast Dairies and as part of modernisation the horse-drawn milk carts were phased out. In 1961 the head groom at the Stratton Road stables said he thought there would always be a few horses kept on because they were so reliable, but in January 1963 Horace, the last horse, went into retirement. He had been a particular favourite, being cunning enough to unbolt his stable and get out to switch on the electric lights.

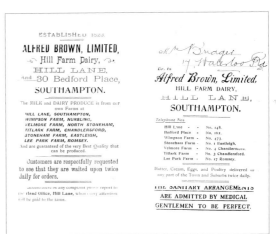

Southampton City Archives
Customer Account book of April-November 1913. This lists the produce available from the Hill Farm Dairy. Infants and invalids' milk delivered by special van in sealed sanitary bottles. New milk, special milk, best fresh butter, best Dorset butter, best cooking butter, new laid eggs, cooking eggs, cream, cream cheese, poultry, Bath and other sausages, mineral water, fruits.

Springhill Tennis Club used part of the grounds of the old Hill Farm, having a pavilion and hard courts until the late 1980s. After the milk depot, then owned by Unigate, was closed all the land lay derelict awaiting re-development, which began in 1990. Hill Farm Road and Summerhill Park were built where the farm and village of Hill had stood for seven hundred years or more.

Springhill Court in Hill Lane was originally built in the 1790s, being occupied by Mr Alexander Scott and then his widow from 1794 to 1811. Reverend Crabb then acquired the house, and it was used as a school from 1834 to 1883 when it again became a private residence. Mrs Cameron Hall lived there until 1892 and then from 1894 to 1916 it belonged to the Spranger family. Mr Spranger was the man responsible for saving Tudor House for the town. In the 1890s Springhill house was extensively altered. After the Sprangers came Major Henrici and Mr and Mrs Lloyd. In 1923 Springhill became a boys' orphanage run by the Order of the Sisters of Nazareth. They were evacuated to Sherfield English at the outbreak of World War II and in 1940 the house was destroyed by bombs. In the mid 1950s Nazareth House was built on the site, serving as a home for unmarried mothers until the 1980s, when it became an Old People's Home run by the Sisters.

Although the fields around Hill Farm were all built up by 1907, Upper Shirley retained much of its rural character right up to the 1930s. The land between Bellemoor Road, Winchester Road and Hill Lane was given over to market gardens. One of the largest of these was Edward's Nurseries. In 1983 Mr Edwards described his work there.

Jack Edwards was born in 1901 in the house at Bellemoor Road Nurseries where his father ran a large market garden stretching from Wilton Road almost up to Hill Lane and bordering Winchester Road and Leicester Road. Old Mr Edwards moved there when his land in Shirley was acquired for Foundry Lane School. The two houses between the entrance to Bellemoor Boys' School and the Course and Beecham Garage were built in 1879 and both belonged to the Nursery. Jack went to school at Shirley School in the cramped original buildings. After school he had to help with the work, feeding poultry and collecting eggs were his particular jobs. The Nursery employed about twelve labourers to look after a hundred and fifty pigs and assorted poultry. A wide range of produce was cultivated; peas, beans, carrots, potatoes, soft fruit and herbs. The herbs were sold to foreign ships in the docks whose crews liked exotic flavours and they even supplied a special large-leaved variety of dandelion for French sailors. Some of the produce was sold in the greengrocery shop attached to the farmhouse and some was sent to wholesalers in Southampton and shops in Bedford Place.

SHIRLEY RECREATION GROUND

George Harris of Whithedwood Farm owned a gravel pit on land opposite St James' Church. When the gravel was exhausted the land came up for sale and at the instigation of Alderman Cawte the council offered £1,000 for the six acres to be used as a public recreation ground. There was acrimonious debate about spending this money. Some Councillors said that as soon as they acquired it they would have to spend money on it, perhaps as much as £2,000. Having been a gravel pit it would need to be levelled to make it suitable for recreation and this expense would increase the rates. Others said the Common was quite near if children wanted to play outdoors and anyway they preferred playing in streets and gutters. Mr Wood said that there *might be something in the statement that the Midland Railway was coming to Southampton and they might not be able to get that ground two years hence.* Alderman Cawte carried the day and the ground was bought for the children of Shirley in March 1907.

Mr Wood's remark about the Midland Railway was a reference to plans for a Didcot, Newbury and Southampton railway. Plans outlined in 1883 showed the line running down from Chilworth, under Winchester Road to Shirley, where there would have been a station near St James' Church. The line was then projected to go along the west of Wilton Road, under Hill Lane, through the Dell, across a viaduct over Commercial Road and the existing LSWR line and to a station at the end of Bargate Street. The Didcot Railway Company ran out of money however and the plans were dropped. Shirley would have been very different if the plans had succeeded.

IN A SHIRLEY STRAWBERRY FIELD.

This 1915 photo shows a wide variety of strawberry pickers!

When Jack left school at the age of fourteen in 1915 he was given a smart horse-drawn van to take deliveries around town and as far afield as Braishfield and Timsbury. Cultivation in the market garden was done by horse-drawn ploughs and until a tractor was acquired during the Second World War they had ten horses on the farm. School children in the early part of the century collected acorns on the Common and sold them to Mr Edwards for his pigs, and Corporation carts brought loads of leaves from the lanes in Autumn to use as litter for the livestock and for leaf-mould. During the First World War some of the farm labourers were conscripted and help with potato and pea picking had to be sought from the gypsy and fairground community in Freemantle.

In the early 1930s Atherley Estates who owned the land north of Bellemoor Road sold most of it off for housing, leaving only the area which forms the playing fields of Bellemoor School. This was still large enough to take several Conscientious Objectors who had been conscripted into agricultural work during the Second World War and also four Land Army girls. After the war the market garden continued on a reduced scale selling flowers, soft fruit, bedding plants, eggs, and fresh poultry at Christmas, until the land was compulsorily purchased for the building of Bellemoor School in 1967. Interestingly, the lines of Pentire Avenue, Luccombe Road, Shanklin Road and the roads connecting with them follow the original field boundaries which are shown on maps of the area.

Upper Shirley was directly affected by the Second World War: some stories of this time are told later in this volume. After the War houses were re-built, schools returned to normal, ARP posts were used as tool stores and air raid shelters were turned into garden sheds. Over the years little pieces of Shirley's past have gradually disappeared. Hill Farm became a depot for milk deliveries, this in turn gave way to housing development in the 1990s and the area became Hill Farm Road. Substantial villas at the south end of Hill Lane were turned into guest houses. Edwardian houses above Archers Road were divided up into bed-sits and more recently converted into luxury flats. The Atherley School, established in 1926, is soon to move from its premises in Hill Lane and possibly that site will be used for housing. The Girls' Grammar School became Tauntons College, an Open Access College, in 1994. Upper Hill with its little cottages and orchard lasted until the 1970s when that land was acquired for the building of Lincoln Court.

Nothing remains of the woodlands and heath of Whithedwood Common, or the medieval village of Hill, little is left of the Victorian hamlet of Upper Hill, and the 'Big Houses' are only remembered in street names. Upper Shirley has become simply a desirable residential area, just as it was to our prehistoric ancestors.

My thanks are due to Professor Colin Platt of Southampton University for his advice and for reading my work on the medieval period.

THE OWNERSHIP OF THE MANOR OF SHIRLEY AND HILL
Rosaleen Wilkinson

1042   In the reign of Edward the Confessor 1042-1066, Cheping held the manor for the king.

1085   In the Domesday survey it is recorded that after the conquest in 1066 the manor was held by Ralph de Mortimer. The Mortimer family kept the manor for 143 years.

1228   It was acquired by Nicholas of Shirley.

1272   Roger of Shirley, son of Nicholas, granted the manor to Nicholas de Barbeflete.

1294   Nicholas de Barbeflete died in 1294, leaving a son, also Nicholas, who died in 1311 without issue.

1311   The manor passed to his cousin Richard de Barbeflete.

1329   Richard died childless and the manor was inherited by his widow Matilda of Holbury.

1333   Matiida sold the manor to Sir Roger Norman of Holyrood parish in Southampton.

1347   Sir Roger Norman died leaving the manor to his grandson Giles Norman, who was a minor.

1362   Giles died before he came of age and the property passed to his cousin Margaret, wife of John Chamberlayne.

1391   The manor was inherited by the daughter of Margaret and John Chamberlayne, Alice, who was the wife of Richard Becket.

1391   Alice and Richard Becket's daughter, Joan, inherited the manor at some point between 1391 and 1433. She married Robert Peny.

1433   Joan Peny sold the manor to Robert Whitehead of Norman's Court, East Tytherley.

1465   Robert's son John held the manor. In his will he settled it on his widow Joan and his son Maurice.

1496   Maurice Whitehead died in 1496 leaving a son John aged nine. John did not live to claim his inheritance and George Whitehead, a relative, succeeded to the title instead.

1520   George Whitehead died leaving a son John, a minor, as his heir. John was committed to the guardianship of William Sandys. John died without issue and his brother Augustine became lord of the manor.

1557   Augustine Whitehead died in 1557 leaving the manor to his wife Julian for life, to revert on her death to their son Richard who was a minor at the time of his father's death.

1571   Richard is now named as lord of the manor in a legal dispute.

1593   Richard died in May 1593 and on the death of his mother Julian in September 1593 the manor passed to his son Henry Whitehead. Henry became Sir Henry Whitehead for his services to the state: he was influential in local government, being a Justice of the Peace and Sheriff of Southampton.

1629   Sir Henry died and the manor passed to his son Richard. He was Sheriff of Hampshire and a prominent colonel in the Parliamentary army during the Civil War. After Sir Richard Whitehead died the manor was held by his son Francis.

1684   Francis' son Henry Whitehead married Mary Norton. They had no sons so the manor was left to their daughter Mary in 1717.

1717   Mary married Alexander Thistlethwayte. The Thistlethwayte family retained the manor until the early nineteenth century, but then sold the land to Arthur Atherley and Gifford Warriner. Mr. Warriner was declared a lunatic in 1821 and his trustees came together with the Atherley family to promote an Act of Parliament enclosing Shirley Common in 1829.

1830   The land was sold off in individual lots: Arthur Atherley now owned most of the land in Upper Shirley. The manor of Shirley and Hill ceased to exist.

1930   In the 1930's two daughters of the Atherley family, Isabel Evelyn Pease and Helen Myrtle Keller, sold their land for housing.

If you own a house in Upper Shirley you can now trace the ownership of your land back for about nine hundred and fifty years.

THE SOUTHAMPTON DISTRICT OF SHIRLEY
Philippa Newnham

Shyrlegh, Surlie or Shirley: these are some of the several different spellings over the years of a name which, roughly translated from early English, means 'a clearing in a wood beside water'.

Little remains now of the old hamlet of Shirley, which straddled the cross-roads some two miles north of Southampton on the road to Romsey; east to west ran the road from Winchester to Redbridge and beyond. Since Saxon times there has probably been a settlement here, on the confluence of the Holy Brook and Tanners Brook. Water power from the three Shirley ponds drove a mill and the Domesday Book records that *Ralph de Mortimer held Shirlei with 8 ploughlands, 4 villeins, 3 borderers in 2 ploughlands, a church, 5 servants and a mill which pays 30 pence.* There were also 12 acres of meadow and woods for 8 hogs.

The residents of Southampton have cause to be grateful to this ancient manor for two important and far reaching agreements, made during the thirteenth century. In 1228 Nicholas de Sirlie, who at that time held the manor, and the Burgesses of Southampton, finally settled a dispute over the grazing rights on Shirley Common. For 10 marks in silver, the Burgesses confirmed the right of the townsfolk to the common pasture land on the eastern side of what is now Hill Lane. To this day, Southampton Common provides acres of open, green and pleasant recreational land for the people of Southampton.

Later, in 1290, a kinsman of Nicholas de Sirlie, Nicholas de Barbeflete, granted the water rights from the spring of Colewell in the settlement of Hill to the Franciscan Friary in Southampton. The stone waterhouse to which the water was piped still survives in Commercial Road, opposite the Mayflower Theatre. This water supply eventually became the first water supply for the population of Southampton when it was transferred to the Corporation in 1420.

City Heritage Collections

Shirley Mill in 1819, sketched by Miss Rich of Shirley House.

During the centuries which followed these two important and well-documented events, the hamlet at the crossroads changed very little. A few more cottages were built; old properties decayed and were replaced; the mill continued to grind corn, but gradually the pace of life increased with the 'golden age of coaching' and the advent of the Southampton to Romsey Turnpike Road.

The town of Southampton grew and prospered; fell into recession; prospered again. During the eighteenth century, the 'spa' period for Southampton, some of the well-to-do began to establish properties in the surrounding countryside, building for themselves fine houses set in acres of parkland. One such estate was Shirley House, *within two miles of Southampton* and built during the second half of the eighteenth century, which in 1792 was up for auction at Christie's in Pall Mall. The house, and a park of about 48 acres, were situated south of the old village of Shirley, about where Henty and Clarendon Roads are today, to the west of Romsey Road, just before it dipped down to cross Tanner's Brook.

The Shirley Park Estate, largely self-sufficient, had its own dairy, laundry, bakehouse and brewery, kitchen gardens, farmhouse, barn, stables for eight horses, a double coach house, granary and dovecote. It may be supposed that some of the inhabitants of the old village of Shirley would have found employment at so prestigious a dwelling. William Fulke Grevill took a lease on the property; after ten years it passed to Reverend Sir Charles Rich. The Southampton Guide of 1804 notes that *on the Romsey Road the first conspicuous object is Shirley House, the property of Sir Charles Rich, Bart. It is a substantial, modern mansion and commands a variety of prospects.* It was on the parkland of this elegant property that early development of a significant part of the Borough of Shirley took place: a development that was to change forever the pace of life in the village of old Shirley.

Following the death of Sir Charles his widow lived on in Shirley House until shortly before her death in 1833; in 1835 the house was sold by the son and heir to a local syndicate. A member of this group was one William Roe, who eventually became sole owner of the house.

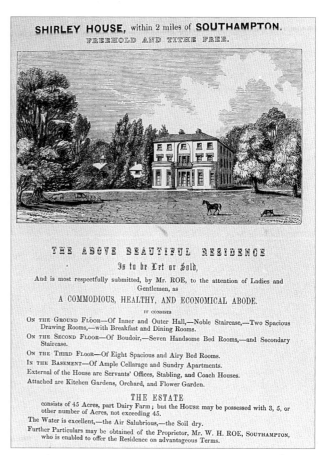

Southampton City Archives
Notice of let or sale for Shirley House, 1852.

In 1852, when the house became empty, Roe advertised the house for lease or for sale. It was eventually let, together with 12 acres of its parkland, to the Reverend H N Burrows. William Roe then sold building plots across the eastern portion of the estate, along Shirley Park Road. Sampson Payne, a well known Southampton property developer, was one of those who bought land and proceeded to develop this part of Shirley. He built solid Victorian villas and many smaller houses northwards from Park Street, across the line of the future Clarendon Road. Until 1859 the Reverend Burrows ran a private school in Shirley House; at his sudden death, the school was taken over by the Reverend Binney, but lasted only another three years. After 1862, the house (reputedly haunted) was occupied only by a caretaker and his family. No further tenants appeared to take over the lease. A hundred years or so after it was built, Shirley House was demolished. The stone flags from the kitchen were used in the wash-house floors of new houses in Millbrook.

Millbrook Tithe Map of 1840. Tracing of part of hand-coloured original. This map was made to assist in the process of commuting tithes (originally payments of a fixed share of agricultural produce made to the local church) into agreed monetary payments. It shows plots of land and buildings. The numbers relate to a key, which gives the name of the owner and occupier of each plot.

Whilst developers were building on the parkland of Shirley House, to the south, along Regents Park Road, established by the 1840s, more elegant villas were being constructed. This wide, tree-lined and gently winding road was a fashionable and elegant address. Handsome suburban residences, approached by gravelled drives and surrounded by large gardens, were built on either side of the road. Today, their memory survives in the names of the roads laid out, nearly a century later, across their grounds. There are also a few large houses surviving on the north side of the road, to the north of Thorner's Homes.

The enclosure of part of Shirley Common in 1830 had already resulted in extensive development in Church Street, and north to Anglesea Road and beyond. This growth in population led to the building of St James' Church. The building was financed mainly by public subscription and the church was consecrated by Bishop Sumner on 20th August 1836. Built on land donated by local landowner Nathaniel Jefferys the church stood apart with only a few houses nearby. The first Rector of St James' was the Reverend William Orger, who rode out to visit his parishioners on a fat white pony; he looked after the parish for 25 years.

The main areas of mid-nineteenth century development were adjoining Shirley High Street, particularly along the western side, where Shirley merged with the district of Freemantle, and around the upper end of the High Street, towards old Shirley village and the development around Shirley House and Park. Behind the shops along the eastern side of the High Street, much of the land south of Church Street remained open and undeveloped right across to Hill Lane. Much of this land was given over to orchards, smallholdings and market gardens, the produce of which supplied the new residents of Shirley. On the Ordnance Survey map of 1868 open land on the eastern side of the High Street, below Howards Grove, is marked as Whitheds Wood (remembered today as Whithedwood Road). To the south of Whitheds Wood most of the land was owned by the business and banking family named Atherley. Their name

and family connections are perpetuated in many streets and properties around the area today. A later Ordnance Survey map, in 1897, shows Whithed Wood still extant, surrounded by allotment gardens. It was well into the next century before this area was developed.

Meanwhile, the rapidly growing population of Shirley required services, public transport into Southampton and street lighting. In 1840 an omnibus service connected Shirley to Southampton Railway station. By 1856 this service operated hourly; at a snail's pace! The horse-drawn omnibus was replaced in 1879 when the tramway system from Southampton was extended beyond Four Posts Hill, up Shirley High Street to a new tram terminus in Park Street, on the edge of the original Shirley Park estate.

Shirley narrowly missed having its own railway station! In 1881 the Didcot to Southampton railway line was proposed to be routed through Shirley.

Shirley Tram Depot. The electric service began in 1901.

Much public capital was raised and the work for the scheme commenced but the plans all came to nothing. All that remains of the scheme is the name of Didcot Road in Shirley, where the proposed station was to be erected.

Despite repeated requests to Southampton Gas Company a supply for Shirley was not forthcoming, so in March 1859 an independent company, the Shirley and Freemantle Gas Company, was formed, much to the dismay of the Southampton Company. A gasworks was built alongside what is now Howards Grove and is shown on the Ordnance Survey map of 1868. The new company made rapid progress, and by June 1859 the first gas lights were seen on Shirley Streets. Rivalry between the Shirley and Southampton Companies became intense during succeeding years and there were occasions where the supplies ran so close to one another that subscribers were mistakenly connected to the rival company. Eventually in 1865 the Southampton Company raised enough shares to acquire the Shirley Company. They paid a high price: £10,500, all but £500 paid in Southampton Company stock. The shareholders in the Shirley and Freemantle Gas Company must have been well pleased with their original investment. In fact, it would have been far less costly for Southampton works to have supplied the gas to the Shirley residents when they asked for it! Shirley gasworks finally closed on 19th March 1869.

Following the Public Health Act of 1848 and the subsequent decision of Southampton to come under the Act (mainly prompted by the severe cholera epidemic of 1848-9) the residents of Shirley established their own Board of Health in 1853. The Board largely replaced the parish as the local administrative body, although it didn't have as wide a scope as modern local government. Throughout the existence of the Shirley Board, minutes of meetings record an increasing number of planning applications put forward for their consideration, which illustrates the great activity in house building which prevailed in the nineteenth century.

In 1881 the district of Freemantle joined the Board; a somewhat unwilling partner, as they had hoped to set up their own board. There were, however, problems with this union; the Shirley Board was already in dispute with Southampton Corporation regarding the discharge of sewage effluent into the upper reaches of the Test estuary. The inclusion of Freemantle, also having problems with drainage or lack of it, compounded an issue which dragged on until 1890, when it was finally resolved. For many things the district depended upon the town of Southampton, where a large number of Shirley residents also found employment. For example, the Shirley Board did not have any hospital facilities.

In 1894 the Local Government Act created Urban and Rural District Councils to replace the local Boards. Thus the Shirley and Freemantle Urban District Council came into being. At its first meeting Finance, Lighting, Fire Brigade and Vigilance committees were appointed. For its headquarters, the new Urban District Council had an elegant building in Shirley High Street, but this prestigious start was the prelude to an extremely short life, as the Southampton Town Council sought to expand its boundaries.

During the eighteenth century the town of Southampton had spread northwards, beyond the Bargate and Town Walls and also westwards to Four Posts Hill. By the latter half of the nineteenth century the County Borough, one of the smallest in the country, had little or no room to expand; it was estimated that only 45 acres of building land remained available within its boundaries. The town was surrounded by independent districts each administered by its own local authority and each with an expanding population, many of whom worked in Southampton. The Borough Council therefore felt the time had come to extend its boundaries to include these dependant suburbs and so made an application to the Local Government Board for an extension to its boundaries.

On Monday 16th October 1893 a meeting was held at which the Borough Accountant was requested to prepare statistics for each independent Local Authority within the Parliamentary Boundary of Southampton, detailing population; rateable value of each District; rates levied in each District; and debts owing at the present time. In addition a request was also made to the Borough Surveyor asking him to produce a plan, showing the Municipal Borough Boundary

The original offices of Shirley and Freemantle Urban District Council. Later used as the Public Library, they still stand at the corner of Grove Road.

and the present Parliamentary Boundary, giving in different colours the boundaries of the districts under the control of the various local authorities and marking the name of each authority on the plan.

Further meetings were held; the Borough Surveyor submitted the plans as requested, and in the early part of 1894, a sub-committee was formed to take charge of the boundary extension proposals. Relevant information was collected from the local authorities in question, one of which was Shirley and Freemantle Board of Health, and the statistics prepared, discussed and amended. This continued throughout the summer of 1894 and finally, on 3rd August 1894, the Full Committee put forward the following resolutions:-

That an alteration of the Boundary of the Borough was desirable.

The alteration should consist of the area of the Parliamentary Borough.

Representatives of the Districts who would be affected should be invited to a conference of representatives of the Borough for the purpose of endeavouring to arrive at a satisfactory arrangements with reference to the proposed extension.

The sub-committee to be responsible for enacting the above resolutions.

There was an attempt, the following November, to pass an amendment to the effect that the Parliamentary Boundary would create too large a municipal Borough but this was defeated by eighteen votes to eight; the original resolution would stand.

Meanwhile in Shirley there was consternation, and on 28th November 1894 an extraordinary meeting of the Shirley and Freemantle Board of Health was summoned to discuss the decision of Southampton Corporation to apply to the Local Government Board for an order extending the Boundaries of the Municipal Borough. This would mean the end of Shirley as an independent Local Authority. The meeting agreed unanimously to send a 'memorial' to the Local Government Board.

Early in December 1894 the Southampton Corporation sent the required papers, relating to the proposed extension, to the Local Government Board. At the same meeting, the draft of a letter to be sent to the Shirley Board was read. This letter was heard by the Shirley Board at a meeting on 5th December 1894. It invited them to appoint representatives to *confer with the Council on the subject of the proposed extension of the Boundaries*, and a copy of the representation sent to the Local Government Board was enclosed. The Shirley Board resolved unanimously to refuse any invitation to discussions. At a subsequent meeting, they further resolved to decline to give any information to the Corporation of Southampton *being unable to see any reason for giving the information asked for*. It was also decided to hold a poll of the District on the question of the proposed annexation to Southampton Borough Council.

On 19th December 1894, the final official meeting of the Shirley Board of Health was held. In 1895 the new Urban District Council would come into being. They were determined to resist annexation and at an Extraordinary Meeting, called on 29th December 1894, it was agreed to retain *one or more Counsel to oppose the proposed extension and to authorise them to take all necessary steps in connection with the same*.

The first meeting of the Shirley and Freemantle Urban District Council was held on 2nd January 1895 and on 15th January Southampton Borough Council made arrangements for the insertion of two notices, referring to the Boundary proposals, in local newspapers, at a cost of £5 12s 6d. On 16th January Shirley UDC voted a retainer of £50 to the Town Clerk, Mr Harle, to engage *one or more Counsel and take all necessary steps in opposition to the proposed extension*. A public enquiry was held at the Hartley Institute, the proceedings being reported verbatim in the Southampton Times the following Saturday, but Shirley was unsuccessful, despite costs amounting to £512 8s 4d; the fees for Counsel being £304 7s 6d. Minutes of the meeting of Southampton Borough Council in March 1895 record that the Local Government Board had approved the proposals for the Boundary extension and *determined to issue a provisional order for including the Urban District of Shirley* within the new Boundary.

In May 1895, the Draft Provisional Order was received, and, also in May, Shirley and Freemantle decided to oppose in Parliament any Bill to confirm this Provisional Order. On 17th June a petition to Parliament was approved at the Council meeting, sealed and sent to the Parliamentary agents to be lodged at once. This new turn in events was conveyed to the Southampton Borough Council, who were incensed and wrote a strong letter to the Shirley Urban District Council. *The Corporation are most desirous that the ratepayers both of the present Borough and also those within your Council's District should not be put to what appears to them to be the totally unnecessary and great expense which will be incurred if your Council persist in their opposition in Parliament to the confirmation of the Order of the Local Government Board*.

Southampton again requested a meeting between the Borough Boundaries Committee and representatives from the Shirley Urban District Council. However, the reply from Shirley was to put the ball back into Southampton's court, by stating that the costs of their opposition would necessarily depend upon the course adopted by the Corporation and a meeting between the two parties could only be considered if Southampton Corporation were prepared to discuss concessions.

On Friday 28th June 1895 the two parties finally met for discussion. The conference lasted for two hours, being held in the Mayor's Parlour; the Shirley representatives put forward their grievances in respect of perceived liabilities for loans already raised by the Corporation and for future borrowings. This included in particular a £40,000 loan for the Belvedere sewage scheme (as already discussed, sewage disposal was a long standing, contentious issue between the two bodies), and the possibility of being called upon to contribute financially to the new waterworks scheme planned for the District. The question of the differential rate between the two areas was also perceived as a real problem. Rates in Southampton County Borough were 1s 1d in the pound; in Shirley only 4d in the pound, and a differential rate of 2d in the pound over five years was not sufficient. There was also the question of the proposals for a new Town Hall; the Shirley Councillors thought that representatives from all the new Districts should be involved in decisions on this matter.

Some of the questions appear to have been resolved, at least verbally, at this meeting, but the question of the differential rate remained an important issue, Southampton Corporation being adamant that it was beyond their powers to alter this.

A meeting of the Shirley Urban District Council on 1st July agreed that their Chairman, Mr Kilby, should attend at the House of Commons Committee as a representative of the Council and, following the meeting with Southampton Corporation of 28th June, *use his discretion to arrange terms or otherwise, if necessary.*

On Wednesday 3rd July the parties met at the House of Commons, and after lengthy consultations, clauses were inserted in the Provisional Order, relating to concessions made to the Shirley representatives. These were: the differential rate was increased from 2d to 3d in the pound for five years; Shirley would not have to contribute towards costs of the new water supply to the existing borough; neither would they have to pay any of the existing sanitary debt or contribute to the cost of the Belvedere sewage scheme or the removal of *that portion of slums already agreed upon.*

Upon reaching this understanding, all opposition was withdrawn and the Provisional Order confirmed. Mr Kilby reported back to his Council and on 5th July 1895 a letter was dispatched to Southampton Corporation. *At a meeting of my Council, held on Wednesday evening last, the members were informed of the terms of the settlement as to the confirming of the Bill arrived at between our respective authorities. As all opposition between the County Borough and the Shirley and Freemantle Urban District Council has now been withdrawn and the Bill will shortly become law, your corporation may be assured that those members who may be returned to represent the several wards in this District will approach the discharge of the duties attached to their altered position in a friendly spirit and with a desire to promote the interests of the extended Borough.*

The Town Clerk of Southampton responded with a very friendly and agreeable reply. It seemed as if the battle was over, a truce had been achieved and

Shirley would move peacefully into the County Borough of Southampton.

Meanwhile, the Urban District Council of Shirley and Freemantle continued in business as if their future existence was not in jeopardy. At a meeting on 17th July 1895 it was noted that they had applied to the Local Government Board for a loan of £1,600 for the purpose of kerbing and channelling *certain public streets in their District.* Moreover, Messrs Dagnell and Co had offered an advance at three and three-eighths percent for this purpose. The Local Government Board informed Southampton of this request and asked if they had any observations on the matter. Southampton Borough Council were extremely annoyed and notified the Board that under no circumstances should they entertain this request. Soon the Shirley and Freemantle Urban District Council would become a part of Southampton, once the bill was passed approving the Provisional Order, and monies required for the improvements would be borrowed more advantageously by the Borough Council.

Early in August, only three months before the date set for the annexation of Shirley District, the Boundaries dispute was once again in the local headlines. Southampton Corporation proposed that the Shirley Urban District make up an additional rate to cover their expenditure up to the final date of 9th November 1895, when the annexation would be finalised. Shirley took great exception to this request and in their turn issued a demand that their first three Aldermen should be directly elected onto the Southampton Borough Council on nomination by the Shirley Urban District Council. Southampton replied that the mode of election of Aldermen was governed by the Municipal Corporations Act of 1882 and it was beyond their power to vary this. The Council also referred to the understanding arrived at between the two parties, at the House of Commons in July, regarding the interim rates.

Shirley's immediate response was to present another petition, this time to fight the Provisional Order in the House of Lords (despite opposition by some council members against any further action being taken). Shirley maintained that the Corporation's new proposals did not comply with understandings arrived at prior to withdrawing their opposition in the House of Commons; they maintained that, on that occasion, no understanding whatever had been arrived at regarding the question of an interim rates payment.

In consequence of this development, Southampton's great fear was that the continuing opposition from Shirley and Freemantle Urban District Council would delay confirmation of the Bill to such an extent that it would no longer be dealt with during the present Parliamentary session and the whole matter would begin again when Parliament reconvened. There were, literally, only a few days remaining during which to resolve, once and for all, the annexation question. Because of the impending 'end of term', Southampton's advisors were scattered far and wide; their counsel was abroad and they were obliged to communicate by telegraph. His eventual advice, on being appraised of the new facts of the case, was to advise Southampton Corporation to present a counter-petition in the House of Lords, in dismissal of the Shirley petition. The documents had to be prepared for presentation at the House of Lords by 2 o'clock on the afternoon of Friday 6th September 1895. As it was by now Thursday 5th September, the Town Clerk was obliged to stay up all night preparing the necessary papers.

The following day representatives from the Shirley and Freemantle Urban District Council met with the Southampton Borough Council representatives in the lobby of the House of Lords at two o'clock in order to meet Lord Moreley, Chairman of the Committee of the House of Lords, who had travelled up from his estate in Devonshire expressly to keep the appointment. At three o'clock precisely, the two parties were ushered into his room and Southampton Borough Council proceeded to put forward their case: *that the continued opposition of the Shirley Council was a direct breach of a definite Parliamentary pledge, given by them in the House of Commons. That having given such a pledge, they were stopped and barred from presenting a petition in the House of Lords and that they had waived their right of petitioning by agreement in the House of Commons.*

In response, Lord Moreley *expressed in very emphatic terms his deprecation of the course which*

had been taken by the Shirley Council and unless they withdrew their petition by four o'clock that afternoon he would report the whole facts of the case to the House of Lords; it was also his opinion that the petitioners (Shirley UDC) should, in the ensuing session of Parliament, pay the whole costs of the case to the Corporation and to themselves, both during the present and ensuring Parliamentary sessions. He would give the parties a few minutes to consider their decision, before he left for the final session in the House of Lords.

An 'historic' conference then took place in the corridor outside Lord Moreley's office. It was immediately clear to the Shirley representatives that the costs of continuing their opposition into the next session of Parliament would run into thousands of pounds. This was the end of the road; they were obliged to make terms with Southampton Borough. They agreed to withdraw their petition, subject to certain terms.

These were as follows. It was to be agreed that the first three Aldermen to be elected for the three new wards in the Shirley district should be elected from either the representatives of these wards in the present Council, or from persons resident in the district, qualified to be Councillors in the ward. Secondly, a clause in the order applicable to the Belvedere new sewage scheme should also apply to the Portswood sewage farm in respect of any future expenditure (in other words Shirley did not wish to be responsible for any costs of improvements in sewage disposal for the new, enlarged County Borough). Finally, the costs of this long standing disagreement should be spread over the entire borough (already conceded by Southampton Corporation in the House of Commons) and should include the costs in the House of Lords.

Amendments were quickly inserted into the Bill and the result communicated to Lord Moreley just on the stroke of four o'clock as he was leaving to go to the House of Lords.

Now that the whole matter has been finally settled and the Bill will in due course become law, it is to be hoped that all parties concerned will work unitedly and heartily for the common welfare of the several communities about to be combined into one municipality, Southampton Times. Saturday 7th September 1895

The final meeting of the Shirley and Freemantle Urban District Council was held on 8th November 1895 and on 9th November 1895 Shirley and Freemantle became part of the County Borough of Southampton. The long fight to retain their independence was over, but they had gained many concessions along the way.

It is doubtful whether there are many residents in Shirley today who are aware that it was recently the 100 years anniversary of their annexation. Today, the district generally known as Shirley has expanded way beyond the boundaries of 1895 but a few reminders may still be seen. The original Council Offices, once so fine, still exist on the corner of Grove Road and Shirley Road, and were for many years the Shirley Library.

Most of the roads laid out by nineteenth century developers still exist, and a few of the old shop fronts. Tanners Brook and the Holly Brook still converge at the cross-roads, although they are not easy, at first, to find, and only one of Shirley's mill ponds survives. Today it is difficult to think of Shirley as a district in its own right, totally separate from Southampton, but in the late nineteenth century the prospect of annexation by the Borough was, for many, unthinkable.

ALBERT COLLEGE, CHURCH STREET, SHIRLEY:
a school and its master
Veronica Green

In the latter part of the nineteenth century state education was still in its infancy. Numerous small private schools catered for the children of middle class families. A full page advertisement for a college in Adams 1886 Southampton Almanack offers us a glimpse of a small and short-lived private boarding school, run by Francis Phillips Cato from 1879 to 1891.

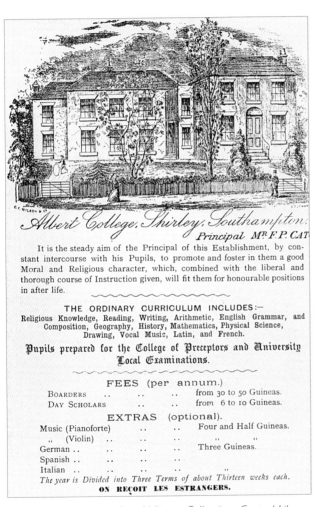

It is the steady aim of the Principal of this Establishment, by constant intercourse with his Pupils, to promote and foster in them a good Moral and Religious character, which, combined with the liberal and thorough course of Instruction given, will fit them for honourable positions in after life.

THE ORDINARY CURRICULUM INCLUDES:—
Religious Knowledge, Reading, Writing, Arithmetic, English Grammar, and Composition, Geography, History, Mathematics, Physical Science, Drawing, Vocal Music, Latin, and French.

Pupils prepared for the College of Preceptors and University Local Examinations.

FEES (per annum.)

BOARDERS	from 30 to 50 Guineas.
DAY SCHOLARS	from 6 to 10 Guineas.

EXTRAS (optional).

Music (Pianoforte)	Four and Half Guineas.
„ (Violin)	„ „
German	Three Guineas.
Spanish	
Italian	„ „

The year is Divided into Three Terms of about Thirteen weeks each.
ON REÇOIT LES ESTRANGERS.

Local History Collection, Central Library

Mr Cato was born in Ampthill, Bedfordshire in about 1835. He married Elizabeth Upton, also born in Ampthill, on the 9th June 1858 at St Mary, Luton. His eldest daughter, Margaretta, was born in Topsham, Devon in about 1862, and he moved to Southampton c. 1865 to take up a post as Master of the Wesleyan Day School. *A good DAY SCHOOL is conducted in rooms connected with East Street Chapel. Application may be made to the Head Teacher.* (Wesleyan Circuit Plan Oct-Jan 1876-7.) For the next 15 years he lived variously in Upper Lyon Street, Cobden Terrace, St Mary's Road, Padwell Road and Bellevue Road. In 1880 he appears in a directory as Master of Albert College, Poplars, Church Street, Shirley.

There had been a school in this building before: Joseph Everitt, clerk to the Board of Health, had run 'Poplar House Academy' there for more than 20 years, c. 1843-1865. However, of more than fifty schools listed in an 1871 Southampton directory, only a dozen survived to 1880. Of forty five schools listed in 1880, again barely a dozen survived to 1891. Of these, only three had lasted the full twenty years, so Mr Cato did well to last ten.

It is possible to compare the 1861 census returns for Mr Everitt's Poplar House Academy with those for Mr Cato's Albert College, 69 Church Street, in 1881.

In 1861 we find that Mr Everitt had ten pupils boarding: four from France, one from Ireland, two from elsewhere in England, one from the Isle of Wight and two local boys from Shirley. Four of these (the French boys) were between fifteen and nineteen years old. In 1881, Mr Cato had three brothers from Wales and one boy from Ceylon. In his advertisement in the 1887 Southampton Directory, he boasts that he *has had under his care Pupils whose parents were living in India, Ceylon, Japan, West Indies, France etc.*, so perhaps the relative youth of his establishment explains the difference. None of the pupils was older than 13. The 1887 advertisement says *Special care is bestowed on Little Boys.*

As for their resident 'staff': Mr Cato was assisted by his daughter, Margaretta, who taught Music. Mr Everitt was helped by two of his daughters, Emma and Jane, Jane being the 'Junior Assistant'. Mr Everitt had two house servants, Mr Cato just one.

Albert College was advertised twice in the Southampton Directory, in 1884 and 1887, and once in the Almanack, in 1886. Although the *Principal of this Establishment* promises a *liberal and thorough course of instruction*, and pupils were prepared for the College of Preceptors and University Local Examinations, he could not compete with the resources of the Southampton Boys' College and High School in Upper Moira Place, which offered *a superior Chemical and Natural Science Laboratory....and Drill, conducted by Sergeant Major Norris, RA.* (1884 Directory). Mr Cato therefore emphasises how *the Domestic Arrangements are such as to secure for each Pupil the Comforts and Pleasures of Home. There is a large Play Ground with Gymnastic Appliances, and the premises are fitted with Bath Room, Lavatory, &c.* (1887 directory.)

High on Mr Cato's Ordinary Curriculum came Religious Knowledge, and he declared that he intended to promote and foster in his pupils a good moral and religious character. In this he was well qualified, as in addition to his previous position as Master of the Wesleyan Day School, he was also a Methodist Local Preacher. In December 1876 the Minutes of the Local Preachers' Meeting of the Southampton Wesleyan Methodist Circuit read: *Are there any brethren to be received on full plan? The Education Department having rescinded the rule that no day school teacher shall be engaged as a preacher, and Br. CATO has for some time taken occasional services with great acceptance, and is considered a fit person for the office of a Local Preacher, we hereby arrange that he be examined before an adjourned Local Preachers' Meeting, and if his examination is satisfactory, he shall be at once accepted as a full and accredited Local Preacher.* And, at the next meeting of 27th March 1877: *Bro CATO has been fully received having complied with the conditions stated in the resolution of Dec 28 1876.*

Mr Cato would have had to satisfy the meeting that, as laid down in the Minutes of Conference 1876, he *had read the 53 standard sermons of Mr Wesley and his Notes on the New Testament.* He was then authorised to preach in the various Wesleyan chapels of the Southampton circuit, from Fawley to Nursling to Bishopstoke. Very conveniently, the Shirley Chapel was just up the road at 40 Church Street. According to the returns of the Religious Census of 1851, the chapel had been built in 1844: it had seating for 356 people and a Sunday School of 118 scholars. The signatory of the return is *Joseph Everitt, Steward, Shirley, near Southampton.*

On 28th June 1881, the Local Preachers' meeting passed a resolution: *That this meeting desires to express its sincere sympathy with Bro. Cato in his severe bereavement.* This was the death of his daughter Margaretta Elizabeth, aged 19. His wife Elizabeth died early in 1886, at the age of 47. Late in 1889 he married Mary Eliza Bullock, spinster, aged 55, born in Derby, daughter of George Bullock (deceased) of Belleville, Shirley Road. She is named on the lease of two properties in Back of the Walls dated November 1890, together with her sister and brother-in-law as fellow executors of her father's will.

By the 1891 census Mr Cato, his new wife, his daughters Sophia, a music seller's assistant, and Minnie, together with two servants, were living at 25 Terminus Terrace, which had been Mrs Cato's home before their marriage. Although he still gave his occupation as 'Schoolmaster', Albert College, now 30 Church Street, was listed as uninhabited.

In 1894 he moved to 207 Shirley Rd, Freemantle, and in 1895 his final advertisements appear in Kelly's Directory: as FP Cato, House and Estate Agent, Mortgage and Insurance Broker; and as Cato & Co, Manufacturers and Importers of Medicinal & Dietetic Preparations, FP Cato, Manager; all at 18 Above Bar. Cato & Co make their last commercial appearance in 1898.

In December of that year he wrote a letter to the Chairman of the Local Preachers' Meeting, in which he expressed his resolve to resign his position as a Local Preacher. It was resolved *that his resignation be not accepted, but that Messrs Morton and Smith, with Rev C. Feneley, be requested to see Mr Cato with a view to persuading him to continue his work as a Local Preacher,* and by April 1899 he had consented to allow his name to remain on the plan as before.

The twelve years he lived at Albert College were his longest at any one address. After Shirley Road, he returned to Bellevue Road, then settled for a while at The Ferns, Anglesea Road, Shirley, acting as Chapel Steward of the Church Street Chapel 1903-4, and as Chapel Treasurer 1904-7. Although his name continued 'on the plan' he took only very few preaching appointments, usually at Church Street Chapel. He spent 1905-10 at 110 Richmond Road, Freemantle, and then took, once again, to moving around: to Howard Road, back to The Ferns, to Hill Lane, back to 110 Richmond Road, to Winchester Road, Bassett, and to Lumsden Avenue. Finally for the last few years of his life he lived at 63 Richmond Road. He died in 1930, aged 95.

From 1891, Albert College, 30, Church Street, Shirley had become a private house once more, occupied by Henry Cawte, builder. It was swept away by redevelopment in the 1960s.

THE HISTORY OF SHIRLEY SCHOOL
Rosaleen Wilkinson

The history of Shirley School is a miniature history of social development in England over the past century. The activities and education of the children who lived in this ordinary little corner of England reflect the enormous changes which have turned us from unsophisticated country dwellers to citizens of a modern technological society.

Many schools were established in the mid nineteenth century because England and the Empire in Queen Victoria's reign needed educated workmen. Education a hundred or so years ago sought to teach children what was useful and not give them ideas above their station. This education had to be as inexpensive and cost effective as possible; schools only received a grant to pay expenses and teachers' salaries if sufficient pupils passed the Examination ('Payment by Results') and the annual visit of Her Majesty's Inspector was dreaded by pupils and teachers alike. Another economy measure was using bright, older children, or Monitors, to teach younger ones. Teachers themselves trained by working as Pupil Teachers in schools for several years, thus providing inexpensive staff, before going to College to become Certificated.

The first school, known as Shirley National School, was set up in 1837 in Winchester Road on land opposite the end of Wordsworth Road. Nathaniel and Catherine Jefferys were generous benefactors of the school. Mrs Jefferys paid the teachers and taught in the school herself, and even bought winter clothes for poor children. By 1859 the school had four hundred pupils and was becoming overcrowded. In 1867 Nathaniel Jefferys donated land on the corner of Wilton Road and Bellemoor Road to the churchwardens of St James' Church and a new and larger school was built on the corner of Bellemoor Road and Wilton Road. This became Shirley School.

As was typical of Victorian Schools, there was a division into three sections: Infants, Boys and Girls. Shirley School served a large area, Freemantle, Bassett, Shirley Warren, so it was overcrowded almost from the start until other schools opened in the area. Shirley and Regents Park were select residential areas and many of the gentry who lived in the big houses and villas took a patronising interest in the school children, calling in regularly to give lessons and hear singing and recitation or presenting prizes and useful presents, or lecturing

An architect's projection of the 1867 school buildings based on a survey of 1903. Made in 1995 by Claire Stoodley, a local architect and ex-pupil of Shirley School.

the children on their behaviour and their duty in life. By 1912 the accommodation had become too small and the building was demolished and replaced with the present three-storey Shirley School.

The keeping of school Log Books became compulsory in 1862, but the earliest one from Shirley dates from 1883. They give a fascinating picture of the life of the school and how childhood has changed over the past hundred or so years. Hardship was very common, some children could not come to school because the 1d fee was too much for their parents to afford. Some had no shoes or warm clothes so had to stay away if the weather was bad. Often children were kept home by their parents to help in the home or with agricultural work like picking potatoes or gathering acorns and leaves. Sickness and death were commonplace, and school itself was no fun, with severe discipline, strict teachers, formal drill lessons and the threat of the dreaded Examination ever present.

Lessons as usual. Attendance poor, measles in many families. Captain Murton visited and took dictation and Miss Nevins took the class for knitting. Standards V and VI commenced their samplers. Captain Murton spoke to the children about stone throwing in the boys' playground. July 30th 1883.

The school throughout has passed a most unsatisfactory Examination, the attainment of the children being exceedingly backward. The girls have done no better in Standard Work than the boys, except in Reading. The writing I am surprised to find on slates. The spelling is very faulty, arithmetic poor and tables bad. More than half the children do not know the multiplication table by three. Every child in Standard VI failed in Arithmetic. English and needlework both fair, but only fair, garments are not well finished. Writing is carelessly done and untidy. Singing must improve. The Grant of £118 9s 7d for two hundred pupils is only just obtained. Her Majesty's Inspector's Report, October 1883.

The Ladies of the Committee visited to award prizes for needlework. Sixteen girls received gifts of dresses from Captain Murton, Mrs Flower and General Russell. Ada Nichols was seen to take 2d from the

school cupboard and confessed to 1d the previous day. Mrs Nichols came up and wished her to be punished, this was done by the Headmistress. November 30th 1883

I, Marianne Gibbard, commenced as Mistress of this school. I find the tone and discipline not what was expected. Major General Lewis came to speak to the children about untidy heads. The girls of the upper Standards have completed their knitting and garments required for the year. Both Grace and her sister Rose Street are to be excused lessons on account of deficient intellect. December 1st 1886. [There was no separate provision for special needs in those days].

Bessie Breaker received second prize and Mabel Chalke a Commendation from Winchester for knitting socks. Major General Russell presented eighty-seven yards of calico and sixty-two and three quarter yards of flannelette for needlework, each girl to have her own garment. General Russell also gave directions about frocks he is to give the girls, fifty yards of grey serge and fourteen dresses in green serge. June 22nd 1888. [Incidentally these are still the school colours.]

Two girls were complained of as being too full of vermin to be allowed among clean girls. They left this week, having emigrated to South America with their parents. January 20th 1889

A demonstration of schoolboys supposed to be on strike from the town assembled here at 1.30 pm endeavouring to intimidate the children from coming to afternoon lessons. October 14th 1889

Mrs Everett called to say she wished her little girl to be caned for punishment instead of being smacked or placed in the corner. February 12th 1890

Many children absent to pick up acorns to sell. October 24th 1890

I, Edith Oliver, took charge of this school. The children have a bad habit of coming in exceedingly late and were so very unruly I was compelled to punish two girls. December 1st 1890

The school has obtained a grant to enable the girls to take cookery lessons. January 30th 1892

Tone, discipline, drill and singing are admirable. Special praise is deserved for the zeal and enterprise shown in the instruction. A creditable beginning has been made in cookery and the girls show much interest in this practical subject. The offices [lavatories] of the girls are in a neglected and disgraceful condition. They must at once be enlarged and repaired, properly flushed and drained and each closet must have a separate door and ventilation. Her Majesty's Inspector's Report, 1892

Mr Chandler the Attendance Officer takes the names of the absentees each week but it seems to do very little good. Every time there is a circus or fair in the vicinity the children do not come to school. We are trying to encourage attendance by putting a Union Jack over the class that gets the highest percentage each week. I am giving a lesson in laying tea on Friday afternoons and those who have been punctual all the week are to take tea. June 18th 1894

Ethel Fray, Pupil Teacher, is to give Object Lessons to the children on the following subjects on Mondays and Wednesdays:-
Volcanoes Cats Finger nails Stitching
England (physical) Singing Dried Fruit
Making Tea Flannel patching. October 15th 1894

Received two gross of poles for use in Boys' Drill. Major General Lewis has military drill in the playground on Wednesdays. The movements are made with smartness and precision, the lads take great delight in these exercises. Songs for the term are to be 'The Star of Peace' and 'Give me a man with an earnest aim'. Poems to be learned this term are 'The Child's first grief' and 'The dog at his master's grave'. May 20th 1895

Map drawing has been commenced today. This trains the eye, hand and brain whilst strengthening habits of order, neatness, exactitude and perseverance. The lads do arithmetic £ s d and farthings, up to ten lines deep. Great interest is shown in metric weights and measures and decimal systems of money. I fear the result of the Scripture Examination was not satisfactory. 'The boys' understanding of the Ten Commandments is rather superficial'. December 13th 1896

In our cookery lessons the girls are being shown how to use up the remains of a cold joint of beef with very

little expenditure, even the gristle is being made use of. The object of to-days lesson is to teach the girls that nothing need or should be wasted. The girls have also received instruction in the making of herring pie, boiled sheep's head, haricot mutton, baked hearts, blackcurrant jam and baked custard. Mr Weston of Misselbrook and Weston gave the school a case of specimens to illustrate domestic economy lessons. March 20th 1898

The Headmaster of the Boys' Department, Mr Walter Rolfe has been master for forty-four years but he is no longer able to cope with his duties and should be replaced by a younger, more energetic teacher. Her Majesty's Inspector's Report, October 1899

Boys in the upper classes are fast leaving for work as soon as they attain the age of thirteen and some attempt to do so before they have reached the legal age. February 19th 1900

Our Grant for each child this year is 23s 3d, a total grant of £306 2s 9d being made to the school. An Aid Grant of £15 has been made available for whitewashing the classrooms and £45 for new desks.

Our scheme of instruction for the year is as follows:-
English   Arithmetic   Needlework

Object lessons in:-
Elementary Science and Geography
Singing   Physical Exercises   Domestic Economy

History stories to be studied are:-
Boadicea   Alfred the Great
King Canute   The Battle of Hastings
The Crusades   The Spanish Armada
Queen Victoria and the British Empire
February 25th 1900

A holiday to celebrate the relief of Mafeking [Boer War]. May 25th 1900

Willmore was punished for threatening to kick his teacher, Miss Wallis. A library of one hundred and fifty books has been established hoping it may counteract and take place of the many 'Penny Dreadfuls' so pernicious at the present time to the lads of the rising generation. September 20th 1900

Sadly the Pupil Teacher, Mr Lee-Scott is unable to

cope with Standard IV, he is in delicate health and his eyesight is failing very much. He is to leave at the end of the month. Vandalism in the school, three panes of glass were broken and one blackboard ruler broken, a boy confessed. October 14th 1900

School closed for the funeral of Queen Victoria. February 1st 1902

Foundry Lane School opened. This has given us relief from our severe overcrowding. There was room for two hundred and eight girls, but three hundred were on the register. There are now eighty children in Standard I and fifty in Standard II: neither has a certificated teacher. September 1st 1902

Weather very cold and snowing yesterday. Yesterday the temperature in the classroom was only 40 degrees. Mr Prydderch is absent today with rheumatism in his neck. January 17th 1905

The ventilation in the classrooms is very poor. I found the large room terribly stuffy and with a disagreeable smell. The infants have to rest slates on their knees seated in a gallery without seats or desks. His Majesty's Inspector's Report June 1906

Miss Gardiner left to get married after eight years of service. She was presented with a set of silver teaspoons and sugar tongs and a jam spoon. November 30th 1909

The accommodation is severely overcrowded. Partitions are needed between classes in the large room, the walls and woodwork of the lavatories are dirty. The playground is wet and badly drained, often the children cannot have drill. New classrooms are needed. Relief is hoped for when Western School is enlarged. There are sixty pupils in two classes, the smallest is forty-five. His Majesty's Inspector's Report, October 1909

The school has been handed over to the Local Education Authority from the control of the Church Schools. December 1st 1911

In the Easter Holidays the classrooms are to be demolished to make room for more buildings. £2 2s 6d has been collected for the Titanic Fund. April 30th 1912

The foundation stone of the new building was laid by the Mayor of Southampton. June 13th 1912

School opened in the new building. There are gas fires for the classrooms and an incandescent burner to illuminate the teacher's desk. Union Castle Steamship company presented two beautiful pictures and six towels. Ink trays have been acquired and even blinds for south-west facing windows. The floor of the Head's room is stained and polished. January 13th 1913

Mr Councillor Cheverton gave an address to the boys on 'Why we went to war.' The teacher in charge of 1B works very earnestly but his disciplinary powers are not strong and the methods he employs are not suitable for the training of such backward boys. When the Head called the attention of Mr Edwards to the great noise made by his class, by his manner he infers that the Head Master has no right to speak to him in front of the class and acts in an extraordinary manner when spoken to. There are four hundred and sixteen boys on the roll. October 21st 1914

Mr Edwards has joined Queen Victoria's Rifles. Mr Chafen joined the RAMC. Mr Barnes, Mr Davis (aged 33) Mr Just (aged 33) and Mr Dibben (aged 32) have all been called to the colours. October 1915

The Reverend Spencer thanked the girls for gifts they sent for the soldiers. Miss McCarraher nurses wounded Belgian soldiers on Saturdays at the hospital, we have held sales of work at school to raise money for these unfortunate men and sent £7 2s 1d. Money for the French Relief Fund of £3 1s 1d has been raised by the girls painting small French flags and selling them at 1d each. A collection of 15 cwt of vegetables has been sent to the British Fleet from school and one hundred and sixty nine eggs for wounded soldiers sent to the National Egg Association. August 17 1915

J Snelgrove, an 'old boy' home on leave from France visited the school. A demonstration lesson in washing and dressing a baby was given to the girls. The baby, a girl aged one month, was kindly lent by one of the parents. July 12th 1917

School closed as teachers were required for clerical work re National Rationing. February 22nd 1918

Holiday in afternoon in consequence of acceptance by Germany of Armistice Terms. The National Anthem was sung and three cheers given for the King and Queen and the Allies and for the women who *have worked so well. It is hoped that the efforts of the teachers will result in the moral development of the children as will fit them to take their part in the great work which awaits the nation in the coming years.* November 11th 1918

There have been very many cases of influenza among staff and pupils. November 1918

Harry House not present on account of being hurt by a motor car on his way to school. January 30th 1919

Harry House has died and his name has been taken off the register. February 3rd 1919

After the First World War schools began to take more responsibility for the health of the children and school medicals were introduced. Perhaps the poor physical condition of many conscripted troops brought about a realisation that the health of the nation was not as good as it should be.

Medical Inspection by Dr Mary Bunting 1919
Present in school:-
1 partially blind
1 deaf and dumb
1 feebleminded
2 epileptics
2 cripples
7 tubercular lungs
several impetigo cases

80 children from Hollybrook Orphanage attend and there is a higher proportion of subnormal among them.

It is a pity it is not possible to make a small class where these children could have more individual attention.

We need men and women trustworthy and unselfish. Strong characters are essential to the health of the nation. Scripture Examination Report 1920

All teachers have this morning received notice to terminate their service at the end of March. At the same time they have been notified that on consenting to a 20% reduction of salary they have the option of recommencing duties on April 1st. The teachers rejected this via the NUT. Consequently on April 4th 1922 school opened with only the Head Teacher present who occupied the time with prayer and hymn singing until the children were dismissed at home-time and the school closed. February 27th 1922

School has re-opened following a satisfactory settlement between the Local Education Authority and the teachers. July 11th 1922

The teachers are greatly handicapped by the low attainments and apparent dullness of a large proportion of the boys who enter the school. About one third failed to solve a single sum correctly. His Majesty's Inspector's Report 1924

Gwennie Matthews has died. Her mother has been sent £1 left over from the money for the flowers as she has a large family and a disabled husband. A list of children in very poor footwear has been forwarded to the Local Education Authority. May 20th 1926

In 1915 the Girl's School collected comforts for the troops, including walking sticks and crutches.

Schoolboys in Bellemoor Road, c. 1900.

Remembrance Day was solemnly celebrated as usual with the two minutes silence and singing of anthems. Poppies worn by the children have been made into a wreath and put in Bassett War Memorial 'from the little ones of Shirley School'. November 12th 1927

There are 319 mixed infants, 512 boys in the Boy's School and 528 girls in the Girls School. Bottles of milk are supplied for daily milk lunches, one third of a pint of milk for 1d is supplied. Received four cartons of malt and cod-liver oil and one spoon from the Education Office for the use of children recommended by the Medical Authority at a charge of 6d per week. After the medical inspection Nurse Cambridge, the school nurse, will pay visits to homes of children re greater attention to matters of cleanliness of a few cases. 1930

School inspectors still called but 'Payment by Results' was long gone by the 1930s.

The school is very well and pleasantly conducted, a bright atmosphere pervading in the classrooms. There is a generally good level of proficiency in fundamental subjects and in Handwork. The children are friendly and willing to talk and a wide variety of apparatus is in use. His Majesty's Inspector's Report, 1936

Afternoon off for coronation of King George VI. Coronation Souvenir books presented to all children. May 1937

A parents meeting was held in the Infants Hall at 3.30 pm to discuss methods of evacuation of children should a state of emergency be declared. September 1938

So war loomed again over the lives of Shirley children. The log book entries for the war years are disappointingly, but understandably, sketchy.

Lessons suspended for an evacuation rehearsal. July 12th 1939

Teachers on duty to interview people as regards the Government Evacuation Scheme. August 27th 1939

Evacuation of all evacuable classes took place. September 2nd 1939

A temporary school has been set up at Hollybrook Homes for some of the children until further air-raid shelters are provided. It is not possible to use our school as it has been taken over by the Military Authority. St James' Road Methodist Church hall has been opened as temporary school accommodation for children living in that area. March 1940

Registers not marked owing to a very small attendance following air-raids during the weekend. Disorganisation at the Methodist Hall due to incendiary bombs through the roof. December 2nd 1940

Both sections of Shirley School closed due to damage done by enemy action. June 23rd 1941

School re-opened as Shirley Mixed, having been occupied by the military since the outbreak of war. Only the Girls' Department building is being used. Some classes are at the Methodist Hall, others still at Hollybrook. Attendance poor after two alerts during the night. March 30th 1942

Alerts interrupted lessons again. Ack-ack gunfire and bombs dropped. Children's gas masks examined by the ARP warden. May 11th 1942

School closed for Victory celebrations. May 8th 1945

School closed on occasion of the marriage of Princess Elizabeth. November 20th 1947

Shared gifts of fat and canned meat sent by the people of Chambersbury USA. Each child received 1/6 tin of fat and 1/6 tin of meat. Distributed apples sent by the Franklin County Horticultural Society of Chambersbury. [Food rationing still continued for several years after the War]. January 20th 1948

The years after the war brought many changes. The post war 'baby boom' hit the Infant school in 1950 and created an urgent need for additional accommodation. The 11+ exam was introduced which divided children at eleven into those suitable for a Grammar School, Craft and General Education, Seamanship, Trade and Commerce, or a Secretarial education. Shirley School was very successful in winning Grammar School places and under Mr Spratley music became an important feature of life in the school. In 1955 an electric tape recorder was bought for the school and radios installed in all classrooms.

The 1956 time-table featured morning assembly followed by a period of religious instruction. The rest of the morning was devoted to the three R's, and the afternoon to nature study, stories and activities, and three music periods a week. More fun and imagination came into education: in 1969 a

film projector and two Wendy houses were delivered. The school was re-decorated and better cloakrooms provided, with hot water for handwashing, and extra radiators were installed in classrooms.

The result of the classification examination has been received today. Twenty girls qualified for places in Grammar Schools, six girls have received Secretarial places. June 28th 1949

School assembled in the hall at 1.40 pm for the broadcast of the funeral of His Majesty King George VI. The two minutes silence was observed. The school sang the National Anthem before dispersing. February 15th 1952

Very severe winter weather, frozen lavatories have forced the closure of the school. January 1963

Continuing frosts and snowfall are still making life difficult for us all. January 29th 1963

The boilers have broken down, school closed again. Replacement second hand boilers are to be obtained from the Chest Hospital. February 7th 1963

The classrooms are attractive, lively and interesting places. In recent years the Headmistress has tried to build up an adequate library but finance has limped behind needs. Over the last two years the Headmistress has moved away from a rigidly streamed type of organisation to one requiring greater attention to group and individual work. Experimental and discovery methods have made a beginning in mathematics and science. The three hundred and two girls on roll are beautifully turned out in uniform. Her Majesty's Inspector's Report 1966

In the post war years the logs continued to record the busy and increasingly adventurous activities of the school. The passing years are marked by the same annual events, the Harvest Festivals, with gifts for the ladies in the Barlow homes and the Christmas Carol Services in St James' Parish Church and the Summer Fairs. The round of entries goes on as generations of children pass through the school: the nurse conducted head cleanliness inspections, the piano was tuned, a flute recital was given, children attended summer camp at Stubbington, fire drill today, inter-school netball tournament, swimming gala, football team won the league, Miss Humby away with a cold....... then came a big change.

With the retirement of Miss G Ferrant, for whom I have the greatest esteem and affection, the two schools, Shirley Boys and Shirley Girls, became one, Shirley Junior School. There are 313 boys and 311 girls on roll.
R A Wheeler, Headmaster. September 11th 1968

An informal coffee evening for parents to meet staff and see entertainments by the children. The classrooms have been decorated and there is a giant Christmas tree in the hall upon which are the prizes for this year's competition. It is for the best table decoration for the Christmas dining table at home. December 11th 1968

The last day of term and we celebrated Christmas and our first term as a co-ed school by all going to the Parish Church. This was the first time I had seen the whole school gathered as one family group. December 20th 1968

Forty children leave tomorrow for a trip to Belgium accompanied by five teachers for a week, a new venture for the school. April 1st 1969

Her Majesty the Queen came to Southampton to see the QE2 and to open the new Ordnance Survey Office at Maybush. We all took up vantage points in Shirley High Street and gave her Majesty a loyal welcome. May 1st 1969

Regretfully I had to declare the school closed this morning, a national gesture by the NUT, a strike. I complied loyally and promised that I would not engage in any teaching but kept an eye open for any small child who might inadvertently turn up - many did. November 20th 1969

The new Headmaster is Mr Roger Barrett. My first impression has been one of pleasant children, working with high quality staff in very poor conditions, bearing in mind the educational aims of the newly emerging Middle School. I envisage a much more free routine, integrated day, and non-streaming with the emphasis on the individual. I hope self discipline will replace rules, in time. School clubs began this week, with football, netball, chess, gymnastics,

country dancing and drama on offer after school. It was decided to go ahead with plans for a formal parent/teachers association. I feel that close staff/parent relationships will greatly benefit the school. September 8th 1970

Once again we are beset with strike problems. The transport workers have stopped again. October 12th 1970

School closed for teaching purposes, the caretakers and allied employees have gone out on strike for today and are organising a march in the city in support of their pay claims. November 2nd 1970

The school day has been shortened from 4.00 pm to 3.45 pm by cutting down the lunch hour. January 1970

School re-opened after half-term with the country having changed to decimal coinage. Dinner money was collected in the new form with few errors. February 17th 1971

Our new form of report with less emphasis on marks and positions has been well received. February 19th 1971

A group of mothers came in to discuss refreshments and arrangements for the PTA Barn Dance, their first social event. March 9th 1971

Cleaning out in earnest for the builders to start on the 26th, the first clearout for thirty years. The rubbish is unbelievable but it must go. July 21st 1971

The builders have carried out a fine job of work and our top floor is vastly different. The new decorations scheme, plus expansion into corridors has brought light and space to the whole floor. We have two fine huts in the playground both classrooms with light and space. 561 on roll. September 8th 1971

Free school milk has been stopped for children over eight years old. September 20th 1971

Fund raising continues, third years are running a French Café with films and a discotheque and have raised £27 so far. December 1st 1971

All Heads called to an emergency meeting at Central Education Office. Hard cuts in estimates and running expenses are likely, a cut in rates is felt necessary. February 3rd 1972

Headmaster absent on course on 'Moral Education' a topic of great concern at the moment with the apparent decline in responsibility and standards of social behaviour. February 16th 1972

Traffic changes around the school and local protests. Wilton Road has been closed off except for buses. We are better off but the residents are most annoyed. May 24th 1973

The end of a good year with considerable progress as a Middle School, but oh the frustrations of overcrowding and lack of facilities. It is now seventeen years since the first floor was painted. July 1973

Parents' evening held, subject was sex education and the BBC film strip 'Where do babies come from?' was shown. October 16th 1973

A most depressing managers' meeting, most heads told of staff cutbacks and building work not allowed. Education is facing a bleak future due to the current depression. Yet school clubs are flourishing, French, First Aid, Chess, Drama, folk dancing. A swimming marathon raised money for the Heart Foundation and the choir sang to the disabled at Sembal House. The PTA paid for re-decoration of the first floor corridor and parents painted the windows of the hall. June 18th 1975

Due to the threat of IRA terrorism we now have to hold bomb drills with different signals to fire drills. June 1976

We are in a heatwave that seems likely to break all records, over 90 degrees in some rooms. Some schools are closing early but it seems best to soldier on. July 19th 1976

The most magnificent school show I have ever seen to celebrate Queen Elizabeth's Silver Jubilee. The singing of 'There'll always be an England' against a background of waving red, white and blue flags was superb. June 1st 1977

The year has seen a definite 'backlash' with regard to public attitudes re standards and tests. There is an overall loss of confidence in modern education, which has become a political football. As always, the children survive and remain constant, indeed continue to learn despite changes in the system. On looking back I realise what a unique and excellent school this is, it has been a privilege to be Head Teacher. July 1977

Mr Barrett left in 1978 and after a term with Mrs Smith as acting head he was succeeded by Mr Bernard Slatter. The 1980s were characterised by the boom in information technology, computers arrived in the classroom and before long every six year old was fully conversant with mega-bytes, floppy discs, databases and micro-chips. Downstairs in Mrs Janet Clarkson's First School department tiny children learned to run their stories on the printer where once they had laboured over squeaky slates.

In January 1994 Mr Michael Brogan became Headmaster of Shirley Middle School.

PC Morse, Shirley Schools Police Liaison Officer, spent the morning talking to year six about solvent abuse and misuse of drugs. The school has applied to join the 'Healthy Schools Award'. It will be a whole school approach with the aim that we become more aware of health issues. February 3rd 1994

Miss Sheila Humby was guest of honour at a farewell party attended by over a hundred people. It was a lovely evening and a fitting tribute to someone who has devoted thirty years to Shirley School. March 23rd 1994

Major internal modification and re-decorating. All toilets to be upgraded and the outside toilets demolished. A new designated space for Food Technology will be created on the first floor. July 23rd 1994

The school today became Shirley Junior School. 417 on roll. September 6th 1994

Harvest Festival Assemblies... October 3rd 1994

So that is the history of Shirley School so far. Children no longer walk miles to school in leaking shoes, they come by car. They don't collect acorns and leaves for the pigs after school any more, they watch TV, go to Brownies and Cubs and swimming lessons, play computer games. Cookery has changed via Domestic Economy to Domestic Science and then to Food Technology and today's pupil is more likely to cook a pizza, bake naan bread or make samosas, than boil a sheep's head or prepare herring pie. Diwali, the Indian Festival of Lights, has taken its place beside Christmas among highlights of the school year. Children have certainly come a long way from learning about flannel patching, knitting socks and reciting interminable poems by heart.

I wonder what our descendants will think of our educational aims and methods if they come to look at the log books in another hundred year's time.

Rosaleen Wilkinson

Shirley School in 1995.

PROFILES
John Guilmant and Roy Hawken

TOM H SMITH

Tom Herbert Smith was born on 13th June 1874 to Nehemiah and Sarah Smith of Romsey. He was the fourth of many children, including Percy, Ethel, Nell, Tom, Harry, Bertha, Hilda, Dot, Mabel and Winnie. He first went to a Dame School: his only memory of this was knitting stockings with steel needles as 'occupational therapy'. When he was twelve years of age his family moved to Northam, and later he was taken on as a Pupil Teacher. He was determined to go to college, and obtained a place at King's College, London, 1897-1899, where he was successful in obtaining his Board of Education Certificate, with Distinction, and receiving the Brewer Exhibition in History. He became Head of his year. Professor Adamson, who had a very distinguished career, was his tutor. Tom's daughter Betty later met the daughter of Professor Adamson at the Girls' Grammar School.

Tom returned to Southampton to teach at Southern District School, in Royal Crescent, later transferring to Mount Pleasant School. In 1904 he married Ethel Wilde at the newly built Avenue Church. His wife was a member of an Ordnance Survey family; her father, Major Wilde, a Head of Department. A brother, Bert, mapped the whole of the Belgian Congo boundary. A nephew, Colin, was a teacher at the Deanery School. In 1908 he joined the staff of Central School, where he stayed for twelve years. His first Headship was at Southern District School. He described how Physical Training had to be carried out in the street; the children scattering when a dust cart passed by. In 1922 he became Headmaster of Bevois Town School. Many of the children there had parents in the Ordnance Survey. His wife died in 1923, at 46 years of age. In 1924 he became Headmaster of Foundry Lane School, retiring in 1935.

Tom was a keen sportsman, playing both cricket and football. He also played tennis, at the Civil Service Sports Ground. During the First World War he was a Special Constable. After his retirement he became a golfer and was a founder member of the Municipal Club.

His sister, Nellie, was a famous photographer in Southampton and had a studio in Havelock Road. During the war a bomb completely destroyed the house, where the family was living, and the studio. He spent the years 1941-49 with his sister, Ethel, at Bognor. After the war he and his daughter, Betty, lived in Wilton Road, where he died in 1956, at 82 years of age.

LESLIE STOTHART BURNETT

Leslie was born on May 6th 1905 in Tranby Road, Pear Tree Green. His father, Cuthbert Miller, was the fourth son of J J Burnett, of 2 High Street, Southampton, a well known accountant and stockbroker. Leslie had four sisters, Edith, Jean, Valerie and Phyllis, and two brothers, Cuthbert and Andrew.

In 1912 the family moved to Clifton Road, in Regents Park, to a large detached house called St Catherine's, in about an acre of ground. It was the last house in the road, built about 1860. It had trees round the perimeter, and looked out on to open fields extending to Millbrook Road. Here were market gardens belonging to Mr Folliot, one of the suppliers of vegetables to the shipping companies in the Docks. Adjoining the property, and facing Mousehole Lane (later to be known as Oakley Road), was the house where Mr Bassett, a solicitor, lived. Next to him was another large house where lived Mrs Twiss, very prominent in the St John Ambulance Corps. Bordering Leslie's garden was a footpath leading from the Lane through the fields to the seashore and Tanners Brook.

He had memories of the other houses in Clifton Road. On the corner was 'Ashdene', where the Lomer family lived. Opposite was 'Hindmarsh', which became the Thorner's Charity buildings later. Further along the road was the home of Sir Louis Dane; next door was 'Lawnside', occupied by a doctor. Next to Mr Lomer was Mr S Rowlands, later to become the Town Treasurer. Next to him was Mrs Neville Ward, and later, Mr T Day, Master of the New Forest Beagles.

Leslie, then aged 7, went to a kindergarten school at Alexandra College, in Richville Road. After, as he said, 'I had learned my hooks and hangers', he went to Hurst Leigh School, in The Polygon, where Mr Lionel B Caulfield was headmaster. After the First World War ended he went to King Edward VI School at 13 years of age. At that time the school was located in Havelock Road, near the site of the present BBC building. His first form was 3b, a classroom in the semi-basement of the school. The room was heated by a coke fire. His form master was Mr Bishop, and he received instruction from a number of masters and one young lady. Mr Smith taught him Latin: the class had to greet him with the words 'Salve magister'. In his private school he had received a good grounding in Latin grammar, but the vowel endings were all pronounced as in English. There, he had to learn the current fashion of 'i' being 'e', and 'ae' being 'i', and 'v' being 'w'. Mr A S Arnold taught him mathematics, and Mr P T Freeman taught chemistry.

The school playing fields were in Hill Lane, so games playing in the 'Break' was confined to the playground. This was on two levels; a small upper one, which included a covered-in area, and a larger, lower area, where the kicking-about took place. The cycle sheds and the lavatories were in the lower playground alongside the Kingsbridge Lane wall. There was a large tree hard against the retaining wall of the upper playground. The boys' entrance was through a gate in the wall of the lane, and by the large drive on the north side. The formal entrance to the school was at the south-east corner, with the Headmaster's study and offices above the entrance hall. There was a small forecourt there, and elaborate entrance gates. On the other side of Kingsbridge Lane near to the school gate was a single storey sweet shop, which acted as the school tuck shop.

Opposite the school was 'The Marlands', a town gravel pit some four feet lower than ground level. While Leslie was at school it was partly covered with long packing cases set on trestle tables, which contained the wood and canvas wings of aeroplanes left over from the 1914-18 war. Later, of course, the Marlands site was to be occupied by the Civic Centre.

Leslie enjoyed his spell at King Edward's, with its morning and evening prayers, and 'Hoppy' Gidden at the piano, and the familiar hymns; the Masters' Common Room at the back of the Hall, tobacco smoke pouring out of the door. In 1923 his father died suddenly and he had to leave school to join Weston & Burnett as an articled clerk, passing his examinations. Unfortunately, the Depression caused a cut-down in staff and he was sacked. After several months unemployment he got a job at Chilworth Estates Office, which was run by the senior partner in the firm of William Dibben.

At the outbreak of war in 1939 he moved to the firm of W H Saunders, architects, in Castle Lane. During the war he lived at Brockenhurst, travelling in to the town by bus each day to the office, now in Carlton Crescent. After the war the firm became responsible for re-scheduling the damaged properties of the town and assessing repairs. Leslie married Muriel Cole in 1963. On her death in 1970 he moved house to Woodmill Lane, where he died in December, 1992.

Leslie belonged to the Holiday Fellowship Rambling Club, and knew many walks around Hampshire and Wiltshire intimately. He was also a member of the Southampton Collectors' Club and collected mugs.

WILLIAM CHARLES MOORE 1905-1987 (BILL MOORE)

Bill Moore was born in Portsmouth, the son of Lieutenant Commander W Moore. He began his career as a teacher for four years in Portsmouth, before joining the Southampton Borough Police Force in 1929 and serving until 1957. His first years were as a Patrol Constable, and his first Police Station was that at the Bargate. In 1933 he was commended for his bravery after he dived into the River Itchen in an attempt to rescue a boy, who was entrapped in river weed, and who was later found drowned. Subsequently he was transferred to the CID as a Detective Constable and then in 1939 on promotion to Acting Sergeant Re-performed uniform duty at Shirley Division.

In 1940 he was confirmed in the rank of Sergeant

and returned to the Civic Centre as a Detective Sergeant. Then in 1944 he returned to uniform on being promoted to Inspector. Initially his duties were as a Patrol Inspector in A Division. Later he became Training Officer for the Southampton Force, and this was followed by his appointment as Court Officer, responsible for the preparation of cases for the Magistrates Courts.

In 1947 he was transferred to Guernsey in the Channel Islands where as Chief Officer he was responsible for the reorganisation of the Island Police Force after the German Occupation. For this work he was awarded the British Empire Medal. Returning to Southampton in the latter part of 1948 he resumed his duties as Court Officer. In 1953 he was promoted to Chief Inspector Administration and became Superintendent of Shirley Division in 1954, retiring in 1957 after twenty-eight years of service.

Throughout his service he was a keen sportsman, and played football for Southampton Police from 1929-40, cricket up to 1947, and afterwards bowls. Among his numerous sports medals were:
Hampshire Cricket Knockout Cup 1930,
Southampton Football Association Senior Cup Winners 1931-32,
Hampshire County Cricket Club Knockout Competition: 1934, 1936, and Runners up 1939,
Southern Counties Police Cup 1939-40.

After his retirement he joined the International Synthetic Rubber Company at Hythe as the Chief Security Officer. He remembered the plant site as a pile of mud and grass and could recall the first trees being cut. He remained there until September 1969 when he was appointed Group Safety and Security Officer at Brunswick House, which entailed visiting many establishments in Britain, Scotland and the Continent. In July 1970 he was appointed to the post of Administrative Services Manager, which he held until retirement in 1972.

Newspapers have recorded his many exploits in Shirley and Southampton. Well known by so many, he was admired for his honesty and integrity, serving the community in excess of sixty years. Living quietly with his family in Westfield Road, he died aged eighty-one years, in 1987.

THE FERGUSON FAMILY: LENA, FREDA AND VERA.

Their maternal grandparents lived in Saxon House on the corner of Victor Street and Church Street in Shirley. Their house, shop (a butcher) and garden occupied a large area of ground, with its frontage in Church Street. The entrance to the stables and their back garden was in Victor Street. Annexed to the house was a cottage where Mrs Langley lived with her daughter Millie. Nearby lived Miss Florrie Hicks, who lived next door to Brixey, the Baker. Beavis, the Undertaker lived nearby, as did Mr Hooker, a Grocer, whose shop was next door to the Salvation Army Chapel. Next to Saxon House was Cawte's, the Builders.

In 1926 their grandparents left Saxon House and moved to Stafford Road to live with the family. Their mother, Matilda, a daughter of James Freeman, married Archibald Ferguson, a boilermaker who was employed by Red Funnel Steam Packet Company. They lived in Shirley Road, then at 66 Stafford Road. They had three daughters and a son; Lena, Archibald (who died in infancy), Freda and Vera, all of whom went to Western School. Later the girls all went to Gregg's Commercial School.

Their fond memories of Saxon House included being taken to Beaulieu in their grandfather's pony and trap, picking all kinds of fruit in the large garden there, and playing games in and out of that large house.

Lena became Secretary to the Mayors of Southampton and spent 34 years serving them at all kinds of functions. She thoroughly enjoyed her work and met many famous people. She remembered with some horror the heavy wartime bombing of the Civic Centre, especially the damage to the Mayor's Parlour and her office. She was at one time the honorary secretary for The League of Friends at the General Hospital, honorary secretary and founder member of the Southampton National Trust, and honorary secretary of the Southampton Table Tennis Association.

Freda taught music at Atherley School for thirty years and has been and still is a long serving member of Southampton Philharmonic Society. She is still a freelance organist and remembers cycling regularly out to St Nicholas, North Stoneham Church, to play the organ there in war time.

Vera was a Guide, then Guide Leader at St Mark's Church Company; later a Divisional Guide Secretary, gaining the coveted award of 'Hampshire Rose'.

In their retirement, they live quietly together in Atherley Road, tending their garden and, together with Kim, a Shetland sheepdog, enjoying walks on the Common.

EVA THORNE

Miss Eva M Thorne was one of seven children, four boys and three girls. Her father, Arthur Thorne, was born in Dorset. Her mother, Caroline Amelia, was born in Oaksey near Cirencester and was the youngest of six children. Eva, born at 6 Church Street, Shirley, first went to a private school opposite her home, then to another. before her parents moved to Richmond Road in Freemantle, where she attended Freemantle Church of England School in 1906.

She had a distinguished scholastic career, gaining a scholarship in 1910 to the Girls' Grammar School. She won an exhibition to Hartley Training College in 1917 and became a teacher at Foundry Lane Girls' School in 1919. In 1932 she joined the staff of Western District Girls' School, until she became Headmistress of Woolston Girls' School in 1945. In 1948 she was appointed to the Headship of the new Shirley Warren Girls' School and in 1960 to the new Millbrook School for Girls, until her retirement in 1964, thus completing 45 years of continuous service.

Professionally, she maintained continuous service in the Southampton Teachers Association (NUT) becoming President: also the Southampton Head Teachers' Association, becoming its President in 1960. In 1965 she became the President of the Retired Teachers' Association (NUT) being honoured by another Life Presidency in 1980.

Her other interests were numerous and most varied. As a child she had joined Christ Church,

Freemantle, attending Sunday School there and was confirmed by the Reverend F G G Jellicoe at 12 years of age. She then became a Sunday School teacher in the infants' schools. She attended Bible classes, interesting herself specially in Missionary work: she supported the education of a Chinese girl for Christian teaching. She became interested in St Brigid's Home for training girls in missionary work and almost decided to be a missionary herself. For over 30 years she continued as Superintendent of the Sunday School. She became a member of the Parish Church Council early in the 1920s, and a Life member in 1982 more than 50 years later. She was a representative on the Deanery Council, and when the Deanery Synod was formed she became a committee member and Chairman of Social Responsibility (unmarried mothers).

She joined the Girls' Friendly Society, and entered many competitions for singing and choral work. Their choir once came second in a national competition. She herself gained a certificate for Contralto soloists at the Albert Hall. Continuing in membership for many years she became a member of the Management Committee of the GFS Hostel in Carlton Crescent, until it closed.

Her own singing lessons continued, with violin and piano lessons as well and she gained numerous diplomas and other qualifications. She conducted several choirs but is especially remembered for the Elwood Ladies' Choir which she conducted from 1945 to 1982. She achieved many successes during these years, as soloist and conductor. It was due to her enthusiasm and effort that she become a Founder member of the Southampton Musical Festival in 1924, Chairman from 1963 to 1980 and eventually a Life member.

She was also a Founder member of the Southampton Operatic Society and played many principal parts during her long period of membership. A member of the Philharmonic Society, she was liaison member for Schools; she was also the musical advisor to the Wayfarers Dramatic Society. The Freemantle Girls' Club owed its existence to her enterprise and initiative. In 1918 she formed a club for young girls and interested them in many musical, sporting and social interests. As everyone grew older the club was renamed the Freemantle Senior Club. Carol singing played a large part in its programme and over £1000 was collected for the Children's' Hospital.

She was equally interested in sport, becoming Chairman of the Southampton Netball Association in 1926 and continuing till 1980. She received the 'Longlife Medal' of the All England Netball Association. She represented this body on the Southampton Juvenile Organisation Committee from 1919 till 1945, when it became the Youth Organisations Committee. Later she became its Chairman for three years. She took part in several BBC performances as an amateur singer. She joined the National Savings in Southampton at the beginning of the war and became an Executive Committee member also chairman of the Schools Committee; later a vice President.

RODNEY ('DICK') TEAGUE Roy Hawken

Rodney was born in 1903, the elder of two brothers. His father was the Steward of the Infirmary, and, as such, was responsible for administration in all matters non-medical. Attached to the hospital was a farm of some 80 acres producing vegetables, and supporting a herd of some 150-200 pigs. Dick remembers this number because, he says, when the Guardians visited the farm and hospital they always asked him how many pigs were currently resident. Their house in Chilworth Road, now Tremona Road, is still standing and used in an administrative capacity connected with the Hospital. Dale Road, at that time Hoars Hill, was a gravel road.

Dick was happy enough, having the run of the farm, and was obviously well thought of by the farm bailiff, who had a set of 'farm tools' made to size for him. Schooldays saw him at Western School. No school buses, so it was Shanks' Pony. At that time the boys of The Seamen's Orphanage also attended Western School, and it was Dick's habit to march along with them for company. Warren Avenue was then an avenue of chestnut trees, and The Icehouse public house was actually an icehouse. With the building of Regents Park School the Orphanage boys were transferred there from Western School. Dick saw no point in walking to Western when Regents Park was nearer, so 'I just turned up with them; nobody said anything, and there I stayed until I left school'.

His first job was at Pirelli's, in the office. He was keen to join the Royal Flying Corps, passed and was accepted, but changed his mind for his mother's sake. Dick was apprenticed to Lankesters as a Brass Fitter and Turner at 7/6d per week but was sacked at the end of his 'time'. He worked for Harlands, and at the hospital in the engineering department. He did eight trips to New York on the Homeric, but didn't enjoy them too much. After his brief period at sea he worked for Dibbens, spending summer with motor mowers, and in winter working in the radio department. World War II saw Home Guard duty and employment with West's Electrical servicing radios for the blind. He eventually became self-employed and had a radio shop in Foundry Lane. Dick was actively involved with Shirley Working Men's Club; he was President for five years, and much involved with the move from Church Street to the present location in Victor Street.

He was married in 1929, when his father had retired, and his mother had died, so Dick and his wife, Ivy, lived with Dad in Foundry Lane. Dick, now sadly a widower, has now moved to Littlehampton to live with his niece, and to the best of my knowledge, apart from mobility problems, is still in good shape.

THE REVEREND JAMES CRABB, WILLIAM SHAYER, AND THE GYPSIES
Rosaleen Wilkinson

The Reverend James Crabb lived at Springhill Court (sometimes named on maps as Springhill House) in lower Hill Lane. He was a philanthropist, and took a keen interest in the gypsies he met on his walks around Shirley Common from the 1820s onwards. Although Shirley Common was coming under cultivation, the wilder parts were still used as a camping ground by gypsies. This explains the name of Gypsy Grove in Shirley.

At the time gypsies were regarded as *roving tribes, an idle worthless set of wanderers that are a reproach to the police of the country.* Crabb recounts in a letter that *in this neighbourhood there was lately a sweeping of the common and lanes of gypsy families. Their horses and donkeys were driven off and the sum of £3 5s 0d levied on them as a fine, to pay the constables for thus afflicting them. In one tent during this distressing affair, there was found an unburied child, that had been scalded to death, its parents not having the money to defray the expense of its interment.*

James Crabb describes in letters to friends his *earnest desire to make some attempt to promote the spiritual improvement of those unhappy beings.* Initially he tried to set up some gypsies in employment and succeeded in getting forty six to leave their vagrant and predatory habits. Then in December 1829 he established an annual meeting for gypsies in the grounds of his home at Springhill Court. This meeting was also attended by local gentry who provided some financial support. He gives a vivid description of these gatherings in his letters. *Each year crowds of gypsies came into Southampton from all parts of the country with caravans, carts and rude vehicles driven by broken down ponies and horses. A camp of about one hundred and fifty persons was made in a field adjoining the house. The meeting was of an interesting and instructive character, an address was given which set before them the evils of sin, pilfering and fortune telling and the advantages of industry and the blessings of social life. Tables were spread with roast beef, vegetables and plum puddings and the gypsies obtained a taste of the comforts of civilisation and an opportunity of contrasting its blessings with the miseries of a houseless, wandering life. Then a distribution of blankets and warm clothes was made and Bibles given to those that did not have them.*

Reverend Crabb set up a school for local children in his house and introduced gypsy children into it, hoping that they would be civilised by the contact. However, local parents objected to their 'clean' children associating with the gypsies. Attempts were made to set up a Gypsy Asylum Industrial School at Farnham instead. Here boys were instructed in spade husbandry and girls in knitting and sewing. This closed down after only a year or two because, much to their patrons' surprise, the gypsy children wanted to go back to their families. When the Reverend Crabb died in 1851, his son continued to run the school for the benefit of local children until 1870. Thereafter the Reverend Lowry Carrick took over the school until its closure in 1883, when the house reverted to being a private residence.

One of the Reverend James Crabb's close friends was the painter William Shayer (1787-1879) who lived at Bladon Lodge in Winchester Road (on the site of the Homebase DIY store). Some of Shayer's finest paintings are of gypsies set in woodland backgrounds and it seems likely that he got inspiration for these during his visits and walks with his friend James Crabb.

William Shayer was of humble origin, his father being a publican in Southampton. He was apprenticed as a coach painter in Guildford. This was a very skilled trade and formed the early training for numerous provincial artists. In 1819, married to Sarah Earle and with one son, he returned to Southampton, living near French Street. The town was at this time home to many wealthy retired officers and professional men who could provide a wider clientele. He took any artistic odd jobs that came his way, painting inn signs, heraldic designs and copying other pictures, although he was primarily a landscape painter. He

'Gypsies in the Wood', an oil painting by William Shayer.

also painted scenery for the theatre in French Street and many of his paintings are said to have a dramatic, theatrical effect. His wife died in 1823 leaving him with five children. He quickly re-married to Elizabeth Waller and had another five children.

Shayer's financial success was established when Hampton Picture Gallery opened in Southampton High Street in 1827. Pictures by many provincial artists were displayed for sale but Shayer's landscapes proved the most popular. Many were of local scenes such as The Bell Inn at Cadnam, the beach near Southampton, the mouth of the Old Canal Platform (God's House Tower) and gypsies or country people at idealised, unnamed locations which could easily have been on the Shirley Common or the New Forest. His groups often featured a grey pony which was actually a family pet used as a model.

He moved to Bladon Lodge in 1843. It was a substantial residence with stables, a coach house and a three-quarter acre garden. He chose Shirley because of the beautiful skies often seen in that locality. William refused to go to London to work,

content with his provincial life style and finding inspiration in the landscape around him. He could sell his works as fast as he painted them in Southampton. However, he missed out on the fame working in London would have brought, and perhaps never won the recognition he deserved. Shayer occasionally painted religious subjects and in 1836 a Crucifixion by him was purchased for the altar screen of the newly built St James' Church in Shirley. This later became his parish church when he moved to Winchester Road. The crucifixion painting has mysteriously disappeared, but a funeral hatchment in memory of Charles Bullen, painted by Shayer, still hangs over the west door of the church. Admiral Charles Bullen 1769-1853 lived at Heath Cottage, Shirley, and was remembered as the last surviving officer who commanded a ship at the Battle of Trafalgar.

Shayer's second wife Elizabeth died in 1866. In 1870 he began to go blind so he had to give up painting. As his health declined he was cared for in his last years by his sister-in-law Harriet Waller. She died in 1877 and was buried alongside her sister Elizabeth in St James' Churchyard. William Shayer died 21st December 1879 at the age of ninety two and was also buried in the churchyard beside the north wall of the church. An obituary in the Hampshire Independent Newspaper states that *He had not painted for some years, consequent upon advancing age, but continued to reside in a neighbourhood very dear to him and congenial to his tastes, esteemed by a large circle of friends for his amiable disposition. Having outlived all his contemporaries he has gone down to the grave amidst the profound respect of later generations than his own.*

His sons Charles and Henry were also notable painters in their day, and were buried near their father. Their headstone reads *In memory of Henry Thring Shayer who died December 8th 1894 aged 70 also of Charles Waller Shayer, brother of the above who died February 11th 1914 aged 88.* Their headstone has been moved from the grave and is in a line over on the south side of the churchyard.

STREET NAME CHANGES IN SHIRLEY AND FREEMANTLE
A G K Leonard

Original Name	Changed to	Year
Albert Road	Roberts Road	1901
Albert Street	Victor Street	1901
Alma Road	Almond Road	1902
Beavis Street	Vaudrey Street	1901
Kent Road	Kentish Road	1903
Leighton Road (originally Oxford Road)	St Edmund's Road	1924
Lodge Road	Cracknore Road	1901
Naseby Road	incorporated into Paynes Road	1904
Osborne Road	Bourne Road	1898
Oxford Street	Marlborough Road	1924
Pound Street	Cannon Street	1924
Regent Street	Redcar Street	1903
Russell Street	Randolph Street	1903
(Police) Station Road	Stratton Road	1903
Union Road, Freemantle	Cawte Road	1903
Union Road, Shirley	Carlisle Road	1903?
Victoria Road	Beatrice Road	1924
Wellington Road	Wolseley Road	1903

REMINISCENCES OF 360/364 SHIRLEY ROAD
Reg Macdonald

Walking through Shirley Road towards the main shopping area and Romsey Road, one passes the Rising Sun public house and the adjoining display of new and second-hand cars. This site (360, 362 and 364 Shirley Road) was originally residential, having large Georgian bow-fronted houses which were set well back from the road. In late Victorian times these were occupied by doctors and business people who employed servants and other helpers for their trade.

In the late 1920s changes took place; number 362 was purchased by the British Legion, who altered the ground floor of the premises to make it suitable for use as a social club. In 1930 it became known as the Shirley Central Club. At about this time the Marlands area, the present-day site of the Civic Centre, was being prepared for road changes. This

necessitated Selby's Garage at 12/14 Havelock Road vacating their premises. Mr Edward Selby, the proprietor, decided that number 362 would be an ideal site for his business, so in 1936/7 he purchased first this house, and later 364 Shirley Road. The firm operated as Vauxhall dealers and subsequently became Singer agents. During World War II this garage was commandeered by the Ministry of Transport as a vehicle repair and conversion centre. Army lorries and fire tenders were reconditioned here for further use. At the cessation of war normal business was resumed.

Meanwhile the Brixey brothers became well known in the area. George had bakery premises in Shirley (Shirley Road and Church Street), and Reg had car sales premises at 9-10 St Mary Street. In 1921 Reg had started in a small way in the St

Reg Macdonald

Ford cars on the forecourt of the new South Hants Motor Company at 362/4 Shirley Road. Note that the showroom incorporates part of a nineteenth century house.

Mary's area of the town. As business increased he moved across the road to larger premises built on Deanery ground, between the Central and Deanery Halls. This was to become the South Hants Motor Company. Expanded business enabled the firm to carry out other work, mainly building trucks for customers' special needs at James Street premises, with tractor sales and repairs at Terminus Terrace. During the 1939-45 war another business, Bell Transport Limited, came into being, having a large fleet of trucks mainly on hire to the Government for transportation of prisoners of war.

South Hants Motor Company was already a Ford main dealer, and during 1955 the Ford Motor Company decided that the premises being used were inadequate for anticipated future business. Reg Brixey and Mr I Whetmore (with the firm since 1921, and by then Managing Director) decided that a site on the corner of Roberts Road and Shirley Road would be ideal for their needs. Having completed negotiations, the clearance of the site was effected. However at this stage Southampton City Council made a compulsory purchase order of the land, having received petitions from local residents against having a large commercial business in a residential area. Eventually, blocks of flats were built in this site.

After this set-back it become known that Edward Selby was to retire and, as there was no-one interested in continuing to run his business at 362 Shirley Road, the South Hants Motor Company became interested, and negotiations were made for the purchase of the premises at numbers 362/364. On February 1st, 1956, a frosty, wintry day, the new owners, the first Ford main dealers in Shirley, opened for business. Since then numerous other dealers, realising the potential of the area, have opened for the sale of new and second-hand cars, and all things related to this trade.

The first few months of business in Shirley Road were marred by news of the Middle East Crisis, necessitating rationing of petrol, which also meant limited sales of private cars. Gradually conditions improved enough to enable various internal alterations and refurbishment to be carried out. After a number of happy years the firm with almost a 'family' atmosphere had another change thrust

upon it. Reg Brixey and Mr I Whetmore, after 26 years with the firm, decided to retire. Bristol Street Motors, a national consortium, became the new owners.

Gradually the appearance of the premises changed, and number 360 Shirley Road was acquired to enlarge the car sales area. A large glass showroom was erected to house new cars, and an under-cover second-hand car area was built. This is the current situation, in 1997.

SHIRLEY SHOPS
by Rosaleen Wilkinson, from notes by Doug Huggins

City Heritage Collections

High Street Shirley, looking north.

Shirley High Street has been an important shopping centre for many years. Businesses have come and gone so that it is difficult to remember what used to be there before. Doug Huggins has written down his own special memories of some of the shops which were in the High Street in the 1930s, 40s and 50s: nearly all of them have long since closed down.

H B Hammond and Son   2A High Street
Jewellers and Watchmakers. Horace Barfoot Hammond FBOA, FIO, Ophthalmic Optician, started trading in March 1912. The business, still trading from the original premises, was entirely owned by the family until the retirement of a later Mr Hammond in June 1996.

William H. Beirne   35 High Street
Second hand dealer and licensed pet shop. Makers of extending ladders, folding steps, tables and ironing boards.

Charles Butler England   62 High Street
Ironmonger. The epitome of the traditional hardware store with stock everywhere, even hanging from the ceiling. The floor was bare boards, but they had almost everything.

Clarence Stores was another ironmongers with a huge amount of stock and that wonderful smell of paraffin and wood preservative and string. They still trade at Foy's corner and also in Swaythling.

R W Delbridge   71 High Street
Corn merchants. One of my earliest memories was of watching the day-old chicks in the window in the 1930s. I became very bored with my mother stopping to talk so much (Shirley shops were a bit like a social club) but I would have happily sat in my pushchair for hours outside Delbridges. Inside there were fascinating aromas which emanated from a row of wooden bins containing cereals and animal feeds of all sorts. This shop kept the board floor clean with fresh sawdust, a good smell in itself.

52

Thomas Brook   76 High Street

General drapers and milliners. They kept a very large stock of everything a needlewoman could need. My first experience of compressed air accounting was in this shop. As a child I marvelled at the long pipes all over the shop into which the assistants fed your money and the invoice and shot it off to a glass-fronted cabin at the top of the shop. After a while, the large shuttle arrived back with a thump. The assistant extracted your change and the bill and dispensed it to you with your purchases.

George Beadle   81 High Street

Clothier and outfitter. This was a traditional men's outfitters. Shirts and woollens were kept in sliding wooden drawers in cabinets, the drawers could be pulled out and placed on the counter for customers to choose. Men were served by men.

William Edward Owen   1 Church Street

Fish and Chips. During the war fish and chips was a staple item of diet for most people several times a week. A good piece of cod could be had for a shilling and a large portion of chips for three or four pence. There were long queues, you might have to wait an hour, but you could enjoy the anticipation of the cooking smell and have a good warm in the shop.

Faggots and Peas Shop   Church Street

This was not so much a shop, as the front room of a house, as numerous shops were in those days (1940s and 1950s). Customers arrived with pudding basins and pie dishes and usually a cloth to cover them. It was essentially an informal and local trade. You had to get home while the food was still hot. The peas were dried, soaked peas. Two shops in Shirley sold ready soaked peas by the pint. Saunders the grocers kept their soaked peas on the pavement in front of the shop in a copper-like stand. The peas were made more green by being soaked in bicarbonate of soda, which would be frowned upon now.

Holt and Haskell Ltd   387 Shirley Road

Sports Outfitters. As a boy I remember this shop being Leek's sports and stationers, where I used to buy postage stamps for my stamp collection. It was taken over by the partnership of Arthur Holt, the retired Hampshire County Cricketer, and Reg Haskell, who was a Councillor and was eventually Mayor. They modernised the business which flourished on the many contacts they had among local sportsmen.

Bradley and Co.   407 Shirley Road

Leather and fancy goods. They were stationers and leather goods merchants and Bradleys was the shop where people went for a really good quality present; a wallet or purse or a briefcase. As a child I was impressed by the strong smell of leather in the shop and it was a place where the very best behaviour was expected. The customers even spoke in hushed voices.

J L Canham   279 Shirley Road

Barbers. As a child getting my hair cut was always a bore. Barbers treated boys as inferior beings and gave them very low priority; but then they only charged us sixpence or a shilling (2p or 5p). Many men had their hair cut every week. At Canhams they didn't allow boys on Saturday mornings. I particularly remember a barber with a club foot and a short temper.

Donald Canham   17 Romsey Road

Ladies and Gents hairdresser. This was more genteel and refined, presumably because of the influence of the Ladies Salon which was upstairs, the barber shop being downstairs.

S B Lowman and Sons

Bakers. They had two branches in the Shirley shopping centre, at 22 High Street and 73 Romsey Road and two others at 13 Grove Road and 57 Wilton Road. This last one was on the corner of Bellemoor Road and was the unofficial tuck shop for Shirley School in the 1940s.

Charlie Ranger   30 Milner Street

Greengrocer. He started out selling fruit and vegetables from a barrow and later acquired a horse and cart. He was a big young man with a big voice and worked mainly in the area around his home. Unlike many street traders, his business got established and he was able to buy a shop. His son Harry followed him into the business at 46 Church Street. Charlie's rough and ready approach and good quality produce endeared him to many local customers and gained their loyalty.

THORNER'S HOMES
compiled from a history of Thorner's Charity written by the Chairman, Mr Alfred Rose OBE, JP.

Robert Thorner was born in 1621 and had a successful merchant's business in London. When his health deteriorated he retired to North Baddesley in the 1680s. Being a religious man and a non-conformist he joined the Southampton Above Bar Congregational Church, known then as Independent Congregation, and became an elder. He was married twice and died in 1690. His will still exists and was made in May 1690. He appointed five trustees to administer his estate, one of whom was a clothier, Isaac Watts, father of the hymn writer. His will provided for a specific amount to his church. The balance of his estate, which consisted of properties in the City of London from which rentals accrued, was to be employed in the maintenance of a free school at Litton and to apprenticing poor children. Any surplus was to be used to build and maintain almshouses in the town and county of Southampton for the maintenance of poor widows.

The first almshouses were built in 1788-9, on a site on the west side of Above Bar. When the Town Council planned the Civic Centre Development they purchased and demolished the Thorner's almshouses, building Civic Centre Road across part of the site. The trustees bought a large house and two acres of land in Regents Park for £5,000 in April 1929 on which to build replacement almshouses. The architects selected were Sir Aston Webb and Son of Westminster, and the successful tenderer for the building of sixty flats was Thomas Lowe of Burton on Trent. The cost was £41,000. The old almshouses had housed 43 ladies, so Regents Park could accommodate 17 more. The moving of residents took place gradually, as the new buildings were completed, and the whole estate was occupied by the end of 1932.

The land purchased included two existing buildings, Clifton Lodge and Clifton Cottage: the latter was occupied by the gardener who looked after the grounds. In 1971 Clifton Cottage was added to the lease of Clifton Lodge which was rented by Thorner's to the Crown House Engineering Company. On the opposite corner of Clifton Road

John Lawrence

Thorner's Homes in 1997.

were Dr Barnardo's Homes for boys. In 1937 the Trustees acquired land adjoining Barnardo's which included a dilapidated house called Clarendon Lodge. In 1970 the Robert Thomas Housing Association was created and West Court was built on this land.

In 1979 Miss McOwan, for many years Matron for Thorner's, retired, and in the next year a house which had been bought for her in Northlands Gardens was sold. Another in Lawnside Road was purchased for the Regents Park Warden and a small office for her was built in the grounds. In 1986 135 Regents Park Road was purchased, adjoining West Court.

The Homes continue to fulfil Robert Thorner's charitable aims, more than 300 years after his death.

THE BARLOW AND ELLYETT HOMES, SHIRLEY
G C Curtis

The Barlow and Ellyett Homes in Church Street were created in 1887 by the refurbishment of an earlier charitable institution. Minutes of the time record that *The Homes were erected by the Reverend Herbert Smith in 1839 at the cost of about £2,000, affording accommodation for 24 inmates free of rent. In consequence of Mr. Smith's death in the year 1876 the premises were about to be sold and the inmates turned out. Under these circumstances several persons interested themselves in the matter and endeavoured to raise a fund for the purpose of purchasing the Homes and putting them in proper repair, and a committee was formed for that purpose, of which Major General Lewis was appointed Chairman and Mr Robert Goodenough Bassett, Hon Secretary.*

£750 was promised by various subscribers and Mr Andrew Barlow generously offered to contribute a sum of £900 on the understanding that the property should be purchased, put in proper repair, and the subscriptions raised be applied first for providing coal and gas for the inmates and the current expenses of the building, and the residue should be applied towards the building of additional accommodation. Mr Richard Dyer Ellyett promised to erect another block of buildings. These took the form of two wings and were completed in 1879 and brought the total number of rooms to 32.

The original repairs were completed in 1887 and an advertisement inserted in local papers. *The Home having been thoroughly repaired the Governors*

John Lawrence

The Homes today. The central, older, part of the building is shown on the Millbrook tithe map of 1840, reproduced on p 21. It is just above the 'C' of 'Shirley Common'.

are prepared to elect Inmates to the vacant rooms. On October 1st 1887 the Governors will meet to elect Inmates who must be not less than 55 years of age, must have been resident for not less than one year within five miles of the Bargate in Southampton and who must have means to support themselves and to live respectably in the premises that may be allotted them without the aid of Parish relief. Forms of application (which must be in my hands before September 10th. 1887) may be obtained at my office. R G BASSETT Hon Sec.

According to the Minute Book, five shillings a week was the qualifying amount which established that an applicant could support themselves

In December 1941 the Homes were damaged by enemy action, but the inmates were disinclined to vacate their rooms. In 1944 gas was installed to individual rooms, and it was during 1946 that electricity was installed in the Homes. The delay was due to shortage of materials owing to the War.

In 1948 the sale of a parcel of land at the rear of the Homes enabled money to be put to use for general improvements and renovation work on the property, and this was completed by 1952. 1963 saw the sale of more land, this time to the Town Council by Compulsory Purchase.

It wasn't until 1977 that the Governors discussed the possibilities of major redevelopment but it was several months before any work was to start. It was largely due to the efforts of Mr J C Cooper, a Governor, and at that time Honorary Secretary, that things proceeded and the alterations were completed by 1981. The architect was Mr G F Gutteridge, MA, RIBA. The builders were Mead, Son & Howe Ltd. On 27th October, 1983 the modernised Homes were officially opened by Lady Romsey. Lady Romsey unveiled a picture of her home at Broadlands commissioned from Peter Folkes, who was Head of the Fine Art Department at Southampton College of Higher Education.

At the cost of £260,000 the Barlow and Ellyett Homes had been transformed from 32 cold bed-sitters with two communal bathrooms and four toilets, into 16 modern one-bedroom flats with their own kitchens and bathrooms. The building had also been completely re-wired and a new heating and hot water system had been installed. The Homes continue to run smoothly today, under the watchful eyes of seven Governor/Trustees who all give freely of their time and efforts for the well-being of the Homes and residents.

CHURCH LADS BRIGADE
John Guilmant

The Headquarters, in an old brewery, was in Stratton Road, at one time called Station Road, between Albert Street and Wordsworth Road. It was opened in 1912 before the first world war by 'Colonel' Claude Ashby and was attached to St James' Parish Church. The Vicar, the Reverend H Bates, a tall man, club-footed and very interested in the well-being of the lads, was its Padre.

Notable among the families involved were the Harls, the Hendys, the Pratts and the Fairs.

The band often paraded through the streets and attended church parades. One of the buglers was Jim Dengate, who dictated some of these notes to me before his death in 1994.

The Club had its own rifle range, a full sized billiards table, a gymnasium and stage. There was a private chapel and quiet room, a canteen and a boxing ring. Cross country running was encouraged. The course followed along Wordsworth Road to Winchester Road, up through Lordswood (which is now known as the Sports Centre) along the bridle path, down Tremona Road past the Infirmary to Dale Road and on to Winchester Road and home, where hot showers were provided.

In the summer Colonel Ashby organised night hikes through the New Forest, finishing up about 5.30 am at a large tent with dixies of hot cocoa. A cycle ride home followed. There was the annual camp with Church Lads Brigades from all over the country at Golden Hill Fort on the Isle of Wight. The Officer i/c was a Colonel Faulkner. One of Jim's memories was sounding the Last Post in the little 'tin' church at St Peter's Maybush at the Armistice Service.

In 1935 Colonel Ashby turned the Brigade into a Boys Club. During the war, the Club was named after its founder, became a mixed club and had an its first full time voluntary leader Mr Reg Burns. After the war in 1949 Claude Ashby gave the premises to the LEA, who received it with the provision that they would appoint a full time leader and encourage community use of the premises. Mr Burns resigned and Mr Arthur Hole was appointed in 1950. He stayed in that post for twenty years. His wife was also involved as a part-time leader in the club. During these years the Club continued to flourish. Alas, because of an electrical fault, it burned down to the ground in 1968. For a time the Club functioned in the old Shirley library and increased its numbers and popularity. In fact, many left the old Freemantle Club, once the Dockland Settlement Club, to join Ashby Club. In 1970 the Club closed, and all moved to the new HQ at the Stratton Road site.

Records show that this Club was one of the city's foremost Centres, surviving a fire and changes of policy. With the death of the founder, the Club became one of the first Council Youth Clubs. Claude Ashby helped the Chief Education Officer, F L Freeman, to found the Southampton Juvenile Organisations Committee. Exploratory meetings were held in 1928 and in January 1929 an Executive Committee was formed with representatives from all recognised youth organisations.

The work of this organisation flourished and was recognised nationally. In 1937 Claude Ashby was awarded the CBE for his efforts on behalf of youth in Southampton.

FIFTY YEARS OF ST JAMES' ROAD METHODIST CHURCH
An edited extract from the Golden Jubilee booklet of the St James' Road Methodist Church, Shirley (1977)

At the turn of the nineteenth century Shirley was a small settlement on the Turnpike road to Romsey, cut off from Hill Lane by fields. As the century progressed the population of the area steadily grew, and churches, chapels and meeting houses of various denominations were opened to meet the needs of the people.

In 1843 a Wesleyan Church was erected in Church Street, a building later used by the Salvation Army until the flats were erected. In 1867, in Stratton Road near the present Wordsworth First School, a tiny Bible Christian Church was opened. This lasted for some eighty years. A third church, built in 1868, was the Primitive Methodist Church in Oriental Street, swept away in 1960 when the high-rise flats were erected.

The Millbrook and Freemantle areas were also expanding, and two Methodist churches were built. One was in Park Road: started in 1866, it was a daughter church to East Street Wesleyan Church, and on its site is at present a Pentecostal Church. In 1907 this Society moved to new buildings in Howard Road, near its junction with Shirley Road. The other church, that of Freemantle Primitive Methodist Society, was in Richmond Road but moved to Shirley Road in 1909. It was built where Freemantle United Reformed Church now stands, for the building was destroyed by bombing in the last war (as was that of Freemantle Congregational Church, near the traffic lights at the junction of Shirley Road and Waterloo Road).

In the nineteen twenties there was a great deal of building on the fields and gravel pits of Shirley. Accommodation at Howard Road and Church Street was utterly inadequate both for the increased membership and the opportunities and need for Youth Work, so in 1925 these two Societies decided to unite, if a suitable site for a new church could be found, and to build premises adequate for current and future needs. Mr Joseph Rank (of Rank Mills) when approached by the Superintendent Minister, Reverend Alfred Bingham, was impressed by this forward-looking plan and promised £10,000, a huge sum of money in those days.

The St James' Road site was purchased in 1926 and the Trustees of the two churches had a series of meetings when various plans were considered, amended or discarded. The Foundation Stone was laid on 23rd March, 1927, and the church was opened on 10th October, 1928, 'to the joy of those who had worked, prayed and sacrificed for that day'. Before this time the officers of the two churches had resigned and new officers were elected from the two Societies. The cost of the building was £3,000 more than the original estimate of £20,000, but the Connexional Committee made first a grant of £500 and later a loan and further grants, the Capital Debt being extinguished in 1955.

John Lawrence

St James' Road Methodist Church (1997 photo).

58

This then is the setting in which the Church was opened. That it filled a need was soon shown, for the membership increased and the Graded Sunday School quickly had four hundred members with a waiting list, while Junior Church was formed, meeting on Sunday mornings. With Methodist Union in 1932, St James' Road came into closer contact with other Methodist churches, and in 1933 St James' Circuit was formed from the former Wesleyan and United Methodist Churches. In 1937 the former Primitive Methodist Churches and the Central Hall joined in to form the Southampton Circuit. In July 1949 the church in Stratton Road closed and many of the members joined St James' Road. Some of the members of the blitzed church in Shirley Road, and later, those from Oriental Street, also joined.

Up to the war Society Classes, the Church Fellowship, the Sisterhood and Wesley Guild flourished. In the Sunday School there were Training Classes for young teachers, together with morning Junior Church, while in the afternoon the many rooms were used to the utmost for the Sunday School, while the Church Parlour held a Youth Group of between 60 to 80 in numbers. The Cradle Roll formed a link with the Sunday School and Quarterly Cradle Roll services were held. The Boys' Brigade and Girls' Life Brigade, served and guided by a series of dedicated officers, developed numerically and spiritually.

The war period proved difficult, but though the church roof was damaged, a volunteer band of fire watchers prevented further harm and many members gave help in ways quite outside their usual spheres, for many people were evacuated.

After the war normal activities were gradually resumed. Young people returned and became full Members as did many who had recently moved into the district. Much has occurred since those war years, and much has been accomplished. Several young men from the congregation have continued in the Ministry, one having been appointed a Circuit Superintendent; two couples married and went to Africa as Preaching Missionaries whilst another couple have been there in a Rural Training Centre in Kenya and one man went to Kenya as a Medical Missionary. Several girls over the years have married Ministers and are working in England.

Throughout the years the congregation has been guided and led by a rich variety of ministers, who have taken a full share in the Circuit not only financially but in providing local preachers and helpers, Circuit stewards and other officials. Locally the church has worked with other denominations in the Shirley United Front, and is closely linked with Southampton Council of Churches.

ST BONIFACE'S CHURCH
Arne Engesvik

It is certain that there was a Catholic church in Shirley by the time of the Norman Conquest, and that this church and rectory were the centre of an independent parish in 1340. However the parish was amalgamated with Millbrook in 1574 and Shirley Church was demolished soon afterwards. Traces of a cemetery were discovered in mid-Victorian times when work was undertaken near the junctions of Romsey and Winchester Roads. The workmen discovered a brass cross, a bell, a small cannon, a cannon ball and between one and two hundred skeletons.

The initial step towards reactivating the practice of the Faith in Shirley was the establishment of a temporary Mass centre in a cottage in Stratton Road, near the old site of Shirley Police Station. The first mention of proposals for a Catholic Church in Shirley came in Bishop Cahill's Rosary Sunday Letter in 1901. *A zealous layman at Southampton, watching the growth of that most important town, felt that before long a new church would be needed in the already thickly populated district called Shirley. He therefore devoted his hours of recreation to a search for a suitable site in that neighbourhood and has promised to give me £500 towards the purchase. The site which he originally selected has, after many disappointments, been obtained for the sum of £900 and the purchase will be completed on Michaelmas Day.*

The newly acquired property was Wilton Lodge in Foundry Lane at the south corner of Henry Road. It was a big, white house of Georgian design in a large garden. The new St Boniface Mission was opened by Bishop Cahill on 17th August 1902. At the ceremony the Bishop said *I congratulate you on having made a step further and hope you will not stop until you have got a beautiful church here.*

St Boniface was born in Crediton, Devonshire, in about 680 AD and baptised Winfrid. As a child he was educated at the Benedictine Monastery of Exeter. He moved to the Monastery of Nursling, which was one of the earliest Christian foundations in Hampshire. The Danes destroyed the monastery in the late ninth century, and it is not certain exactly where the monastery was, but it may have been close to the present Anglican church in Nursling, which is dedicated to St Boniface.

He was ordained to the priesthood when he was thirty. Winfrid longed to preach the gospel to pagans, and he left for Germany in 716. He was very successful in his missionary work and the Pope of the time recalled him to Rome in 723, ordained him Bishop and changed his name to Boniface. In 732 Pope Gregory III constituted him Archbishop and Primate of all Germany. His work now also covered much of France, and to help him he invited over from England many holy men and religious women, including his cousin, St Thecla. He kept in touch with his native land and converted Ethelbald, King of Mercia, by letter. In 754 he set out to administer the Sacrament of Confirmation to several thousands of his converts. As he prepared for the ceremony, he was set upon by pagans and died by the sword with fifty-two companions. His remains lie in the Monastery of Fulda, which he had founded, in Hessen in West Germany, which has now become a place of pilgrimage.

In Foundry Lane Mass was initially celebrated in the dining room of Wilton Lodge. When the congregation got too big for that, the French windows were thrown open and an awning erected to form a garden annex. The 'beautiful church' on the Foundry Lane site visualised by the Bishop might not quite have recognised itself in this description when a tin building was constructed! When the tin church needed re-painting in 1910, a collection towards this outlay brought in 13s 6 1/2d. Two parishioners made personal donations, and the bill for the re-painting came to £5. It is interesting to note that this kind of expenditure was deferred until the debt on the church had been cleared. That milestone was announced one month before the decorator began his work.

A German priest by the name of Father A Sander, who lived in Leighton Road (now renamed St Edmund's Road), made a donation to the parish of a statue of St Boniface, 'the Apostle of his Fatherland'. This statue was erected at the Foundry Lane chapel.

To begin with the Shirley Mission came under St Joseph's in Bugle Street. Father Green, who was born in Wilton Cottage in Carlton Road, was given responsibility for the Shirley Mission. At the end of 1905 the responsibility for the Shirley Mission was transferred to St Edmund's in the Avenue.

The parishioners' struggling lifestyle was reflected in St Boniface's Church income, and the priest shared his people's poverty. The congregation would try to treat him to an occasional small luxury by putting a penny or two into the plate which was held by the door at the end of Sunday Mass, 'for Father's tobacco'.

In 1913 St Boniface's Mission was granted independence from St Edmund's. The first Parish Priest was Father Michael John Mullin, who took up residence in Wilton Lodge towards the end of 1913. 1919 signalled the next move forward in the fortunes of the parish. By a Conveyance dated 19th December, land in Shirley Road was acquired from Whithedwood Estates Ltd for the sum of £1,200, as a first step to building a permanent church.

In 1922 Monsignor Gilbert Vincent Bull, a priest of Nottingham Diocese, came to Wilton Lodge while the regular priest, Father Shanahan, was on holiday. People in Shirley High Street would watch spellbound as the splendid figure promenaded up the street, dressed in full regalia: red-trimmed headgear, flowing black cape lined with scarlet satin, and patent-leather, silver-buckled pumps, with a dignity of bearing that would have upstaged Cardinal Wolsey on a State occasion.

Father Thomas Byrne took over the care of the parish in 1923. He was in his late thirties and is described as a bluff Irishman of kindliness and humour. There are many stories about his humour. He was for example fond of telling the yarn of an Irishman who approached the Church of England vicar in the hope of interesting him in a batch of new-born kittens he had for sale, stressing that they were good Protestant cats. Later, making similar contact with the Catholic priest, the man asserted that they were sound Catholic animals. Undaunted when the priest challenged his apparent duplicity,

the would-be salesman explained that, since his business negotiations with his last customer, the creatures' eyes had opened.

Wilton Lodge was doubtless rather short on comfort. Father Byrne once got a rather bad cold and had to take to his bed under an umbrella because heavy rain seeped through the ceiling. The roof of the tin church also sprung a leak because of corrosion. At the time Charles Wills lived in Nightingale Road. His family business was the Mafeking Steam Laundry and he lent some of his workmen to repair the roofs of both buildings.

However, the parish was already raising funds for the new church in Shirley Road. To that end, several families undertook a weekly round of the parish, on foot or on bicycle, to gather the faithful's tribute of two shillings apiece, sealed in a small envelope. The Dunlop family had for many years given generous support to the Shirley Mission. Archibald Claude Dunlop died in the mid 1920s and a substantial bequest under his will crowned the efforts of St Boniface's parish. It made possible the construction of the beautiful church that today is their spiritual home.

The church was completed in October 1927 after ninety weeks' work. The cost of building the church and the presbytery was £15,000. Locally the church was often called Shirley Temple, both because of the shape of the bell-tower and because at that time Shirley Temple was every cinema-goer's favourite film-star.

The Southampton Press of October 1927 described the new church: *Dedicated to St Boniface and designed in the Romanesque style, the church is a Latin cross on plan, and measures 138 feet from east to west and 60 feet from north to south across the transepts. It is faced externally with handmade, sandfaced, multi-coloured bricks from the Daneshill kilns at Basingstoke, relieved by arches and brick and tile bands, dressings and pattern-work of contrasting sizes and colour tones, the roofs and parapets being covered with Lombardy sandfaced tiles, the whole blending into a rich and elaborate composition of a striking and original character. The barrel-vaulted nave is broken by three bays on each side, in which are placed large semi-circular headed windows filled with leaded glass of a simple but appropriate design.*

The west front of St Boniface's church, as it appears today.

The transepts are also barrel-vaulted, and over the crossing rises a large octagonal lantern, which lends an air of spaciousness and added dignity to the edifice. At the east end is the Sanctuary, flanked by two side chapels and an octagonal apse, in which is placed a high altar, built entirely of white marble with shafts, base and embellishments of various specially selected coloured marbles and inlaid Venetian mosaics, all executed by Messrs Marchetti Ltd. of Portsmouth. Adjoining the south transept are the sacristies, and at the west end of the nave is a large gallery, Narthex Confessionals and a baptistry.

The west front is imposing, the massive main entrance doors being set in a deeply recessed porch, which is enclosed by triple arches supported by columns of polished Sienna marble, with richly carved capitals of white marble. The main entrance is flanked on each side by secondary entrance doors and porches, and at the north west corner a handsome campanile, or bell-tower, rises to a height of 75 feet above the ground.

The nave is paved with Austrian oak blocks, and the processional aisles which surround it with special composition, relieved with inlaid pattern panels of ceramic mosaics. The Sanctuary, which rises four feet above the nave floor, is paved in white marble, with bands and borders of Swedish green marble. The woodwork throughout, with the exception of the Austrian oak entrance doors, is of British Columbian pine, stained and varnished, and the church is furnished with specially designed seating in the same material.

The church is an example of modern craftsmanship of unusual interest to all students of building construction, and reflects the highest credit on the builders, Jenkins and Sons Ltd of Southampton, and their staff. The whole scheme was designed by and carried out under the supervision of Mr Wilfred C Mangan of Preston, an architect who has designed many Roman Catholic churches.

The original statue of St Boniface at the new church was of oak and cost less than £40. The architect found it in an Art and Book shop in London. It was positioned to face in the direction of the saint's one-time monastic home at Nursling. Unfortunately it blew down in a storm at the beginning of the Second World War. The present statue was dedicated on 16th June 1954.

After the new church was completed the parish did not need the old tin church any more. It had never been consecrated and was unfit to move elsewhere. The whole property in Foundry Lane was sold in February 1929 for £1,100. By 1930 Wilton Lodge had been pulled down, but the old church was still being used as a hall for dances, whist drives and other social activities. It was eventually destroyed by fire.

During the first years in the new church the congregation gathered resources to furnish the interior with pictures, statues and all the sacramentals that make a church the spiritual home of its people. It has been said that various families each bought one of the Stations of the Cross. Several ladies formed a Needlework Guild, and met regularly to enjoy one another's companionship while sewing whatever was needed by the church. Members of this group instituted a rota for the floral decoration of the sanctuary. For a few years the old harmonium, which had provided music for the liturgy at Foundry Lane, served the new church, but later the parish managed to buy a two-manual organ built by Mr James Ivimey of Southampton, at a cost of £1,600.

One of the longest serving and most loved priests in St Boniface's was Father William O'Sullivan. He was born in Midleton, Co. Cork. After having studied at All Hallows, Dublin, he was ordained on 11th June 1922. He was appointed Parish Priest of St Boniface's in 1939 at the age of forty-one. He served at St Boniface's for twenty-eight years, until failing health and eye-sight forced him to retire in 1967 at the age of sixty-nine.

Father Willie had a natural flair for neighbourliness, and was in the vanguard of the ecumenical movement. He was close friends with clergy and laity of all denominations. He was Chaplain to the Docks, did two terms as Mayor's Chaplain and was a chairman of Southampton Municipal Charities. He became involved in each facet of local life. He seemed to know everybody and could stand at his gate greeting by name all who passed along Shirley High Street.

Father O'Sullivan put accommodation in the hall at the disposal of the Air Raid Precaution organisation and he joined the Wardens' ranks. The GPO set up a temporary sorting office there too and the landlord's name was entered on their books as a casual Christmas worker. Needless to say, everybody connected with these concerns was embraced into Father Willie's ever-widening circle of friends. The boiler room under the church doubled up as an air raid shelter. There could be no service in the church after dark as it was impossible to cover all the windows to comply with the blackout regulation. The parish certainly counted itself fortunate that the church, hall and presbytery all escaped damage of any significance when other parts of Shirley were razed to the ground.

During the war several ladies helped to run a canteen set up in the church hall for the use of men of the Merchant Navy and Armed Forces. Inevitably, they would find on their hands the occasional intoxicated customer who, should he encounter Father O'Sullivan, would find the rest of his liquor taken from him and poured down the kitchen sink.

Sunday and Wednesday dances in the hall were very popular. They were originally run for the Apostleship of the Sea, when Southampton was at its height as a commercial port, and a second home for the Merchant Navy. Seamen as well as parishioners and their friends would flock to St Boniface's, and dance to the four-piece band for 1/6d. Even on Wednesdays the dances would attract over a hundred people while on Sunday, three hundred would squeeze in.

The Silver Jubilee of Father O'Sullivan's ordination and the eventual consecration of St Boniface's church fell within the same week of June 1947, on 11th and 17th respectively. In September 1947 Father O'Sullivan was appointed 'Officiating Chaplain Royal Air Force to personnel at R.A.F. No. 2 Movement Unit (E) Southampton'.

The highlight of 1958 was the honour paid to Father O'Sullivan on his promotion to Honorary Canon of the diocese. So now 'Father Willie' was recast as 'Canon Willie' although children still preferred to accept his invitation to call him 'Uncle Willie'.

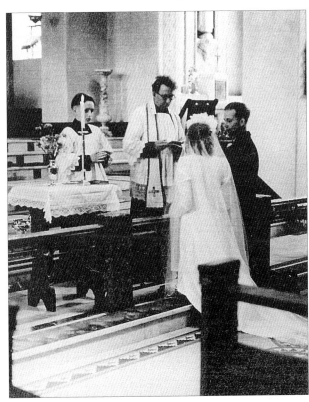

Arne Engesvik

Wedding of Fionnuala Burke and Arne Engesvik on 22nd June 1947, five days after the church had been consecrated. Celebrated by Father O'Sullivan.

Another celebration took place in 1964 in the form of a Mass of Thanksgiving to mark Canon O'Sullivan's Silver Jubilee as Parish Priest of St Boniface's Church. He retired in August 1967 and went to Branksome and later Dublin. He died at the age of eighty-seven in Dublin on 21st April 1985, and was buried in his own village of Midleton, County Cork.

On 1st September 1967 the present Parish Priest, now Canon MacDermot-Roe, took over at St Boniface's.

During the first half of 1967 Father Hetherington had completed the modernisation of the presbytery, hall and grounds, so Father MacDermot-Roe was able to turn his attention to re-ordering the sanctuary in accordance with liturgical requirements arising out of the decrees of the Second Vatican Council. It was an undertaking of importance and responsibility which called for the best specialised advice, and this he obtained from the architect, Mr R Sawyer of Winchester. Under Mr Sawyer's expert guidance the high altar was re-modelled by Vokes and Beck, a Winchester firm of masons. A colour scheme in harmony with the conversion was professionally devised for the sanctuary, and the body of the church redecorated. The new high altar was solemnly consecrated by Bishop Derek Worlock on 16th November 1969.

A Mass of Thanksgiving, followed by a very happy party in the church hall, marked the Silver Jubilee of Father MacDermot-Roe's ordination to the priesthood at All Hallows College, Dublin, on 17th June 1951. This anniversary in 1976 saw a delightful gathering of his own family, his numerous adopted children of Shirley and many friends, offering their prayers, affection and congratulations.

In October 1977, it was the turn of the church to celebrate its own Jubilee. The late Bishop Emery was Chief Celebrant at an evening Mass in honour of St Boniface, on the Golden Anniversary of the opening of the church. With the Bishop were Father MacDermot-Roe, Father Murphy, the priests of Southampton Deanery and several who had served the parish in the past. Ministers of other denominations in Shirley attended, and the assembly was honoured by the presence of the

Mayor of Southampton, Councillor Mrs Joyce Pitter.

In the early 1980s a new hall was built and a simple garden laid on the land. In June 1983 Father MacDermot-Roe was raised to be a Canon of the Cathedral Chapter, and the following October he became Dean of Southampton. In 1992 he celebrated his Silver Jubilee as Parish Priest of St Boniface's.

A wide range of needs is met by such on-going organisations as the Society of St Vincent de Paul, Union of Catholic Mothers and all branches of the scouting movement, together with newer ventures. The latter include a Young People's Prayer Group, Mothers' and Toddlers' Group, and a Playgroup already widely and ecumenically renowned for its excellence. The past two decades have seen parish pilgrimages to Lourdes, Rome, Walsingham and Aylesford. Charitable objectives have remained a high priority, aimed at a variety of beneficiaries ranging from a Mission Hospital in Uganda to St James' Shelter which caters for the homeless of Southampton.

A great number of dedicated and colourful people have worked for the St Boniface's Mission in many different ways and have contributed to making St Boniface's a happy meeting place and the centre of Catholics in Shirley.

SOME SHIRLEY HOUSES: Hollybrook House, The Octagon, and Whithedwood House and Farm
Rosaleen Wilkinson

Hollybrook House in 1838.

Hollybrook House was built in 1836 for Nathaniel Jefferys. It was in the area now enclosed by Linford Crescent. He was a great local benefactor and provided land for both the new St James' church and two schools in Shirley. He died in 1873 aged eighty-five, and his widow Catherine died in 1876 aged eighty-two.

For the next twenty years Alfred Seymour lived in the house, giving his name to Seymour Road. He was followed by John Gaide Dickson until 1910. The Southampton solicitor Herbert Blatch bought 120 acres of the estate, and a few years later in 1902 the Corporation bought forty-seven acres from him. They terminated the tenancy of John Jenman of Hollybrook Farm and laid out the new Hollybrook Cemetery which was opened in 1913.

In 1910 the Board of Guardians acquired Hollybrook House and in August 1912 opened it as a home for pauper boys. Then in 1919 they built 'cottage homes' to take girls transferred from the Poor Law Institute in St Mary Street. In 1955 the Children's Homes were closed, the children being sent to smaller units and foster homes. Some of the buildings were incorporated into the new Hollybrook Primary school in 1958 and one became the office of the Weights and Measures (Trading Standards) Department. Hollybrook House itself was demolished in 1950 and the land used for Council housing. The gate-posts and remnants of the avenue of trees leading up to the house can be seen in Winchester Road, opposite the end of Luccombe Road. The lodge was demolished in the late 1970s.

The Octagon, now 132 Winchester Road, was one of Shirley's pleasant country houses. Few details of the history of this house are available. It was probably built in the 1850s. Its extensive grounds

The Octagon in Winchester Road; modern photo.

sloped down towards the Tanners Brook Valley and Shirley Ponds. In the 1880s it was owned by Mr Sandeman. He was a kindly man who lent his field for all kinds of local celebrations and Sunday School Treats. One such Treat was Queen Victoria's Golden Jubilee celebration in 1887. This is a Mr Martin's recollection of the day, printed in a local newspaper in 1932. *At five o'clock a procession of eighteen hundred children was formed in front of the church and headed by a band, marched down Church Street, along High Street and up Anglesea Road to the Octagon field. We had assembled at Shirley School, the old fashioned one-storey building. While we waited we watched the fowls in Hatch's farmyard. Tom Hatch's farm was at the rear of the church, opposite the school. In those days the farm included two or three mud cottages with enormously thick walls, the last one came down thirty years ago [that is, 1900]. Every day the boys used to see Hatch's cows being driven out to pasture. The shops were hung with bunting in the High Street. Each child was given a Jubilee Medal, there were coloured minstrels, swing boats, sweets and a huge tea in the Octagon field and the day closed with a brilliant display of fireworks!*

The area known as Whitehead's Wood, corrupted to Whithedwood, had been occupied by farms in the area certainly since the 1650s and most likely well before that date. There is no evidence to suggest a manor house at Whithedwood, as the main manor houses were at Hill and Shirley, so these were outlying farms. The Millbrook parish register records three different families living in the Whithedwood area in the mid 1600s: 25th July 1657, Anne, daughter of Andrew Jons of Whittedswood born; 20th August 1657, John

Russon of Whittedswood buried; 18th June 1660, John Neave of Whithedwood buried.

A map of 1778 shows that St James' Road was then called the Drove and it petered out just beyond Gipsy Grove, in fact where the modern St James' Road becomes Raymond Road at the junction with Malmesbury Road. Shirley Avenue was then an un-named track, although later it was known as Whithedwood Avenue. Two farms are shown on this map. One was on the corner of what is now Upper Shirley Avenue and St James' Road and had a cattle pound next to it. The other farm was on land between the ends of the modern Bridlington Avenue and Eastbourne Avenue, fronting on to St James' Road: this was Whithedwood Farm.

St James' Road in the nineteenth century. The trees in the foreground follow the line of Gypsy Grove. The building in the centre is the coach house of Whithedwood House, and Whithedwood Farmhouse is just visible to the right.

The same two farms appear on a map of 1866 and in Kelly's Directory for 1871. Henry Kemp of Whithedwood is listed as a dairyman. Mrs Elizabeth Kemp is listed at Whithedwood Farm Dairy in subsequent years up to 1894, so Mr Kemp must have died in the meantime. However, by the time a new map was published in 1897 changes had taken place. The farm on the corner of Upper Shirley Avenue had disappeared. Wilton Road had been laid out and was called simply

Mr and Mrs Yaldron

New Road and a house called the Red House had been built beside it not far from Whithedwood Farm. This house still exists as 146 Wilton Road near the Bassett Tennis Club. A track which would later become Bridlington Avenue led between the Red House and Whithedwood Farm. Opposite the Red House, in the area of the present Eastbourne Avenue, there were brick works and two kilns. It would seem that George Harris who lived at the Red House and owned the brickworks bought up Whithedwood Farm, because in 1897 George Harris is listed in the Directory as being dairyman and farmer of Whithedwood Farm, St James' Road, as well as resident in his Wilton Road house.

In 1908 Mr Harris closed down Whithedwood Farm and transferred the dairy business to the Red House, changing its name to Whithedwood. The farm cottages of the original Whithedwood Farm were rented out to George Herbert and Edward Toms. In 1910 house building began on the farm site along St James' Road, and in Kelly's Directory the farm cottages are listed between two villas named Homerest and Ardnahane. By 1912 the old Whithedwood Farm Buildings had been demolished, and nine more houses are named, but there is no mention of the farm cottages.

George Harris became a prosperous farmer and builder, owning brickworks at Wimpson and Rownhams as well as the works in Wilton Road and the gravel pit opposite St James' Church. His home at Whithedwood was a substantial Victorian house with large grounds and farmland around it. He died in 1912 and his estate was broken up. The house was no longer needed as a farm house and passed into private ownership.

Whithedwood House, on the other hand, was a gentleman's country residence, and stood where Whithedwood Avenue is presently sited. It was built about 1820 for William Howard, and his son John Janson Howard lived there after William's death. Sometime in the 1880s it became the home of Charles Shubrick Day until his death in 1920.

City Heritage Collections

Whithedwood House.

67

The parlour in the late nineteenth century.

Like many other members of the gentry Mr Day was a local benefactor and allowed his grounds to be used for flower shows and fêtes and scout meetings. He was a great supporter of cricket and rugby, and Shirley cricket club played its matches in the grounds of Whithedwood House. His land extended from Gypsy Grove across to Shirley Avenue and in the early 1900s a large area of the estate was leased to the Shirley Golf Club. A golf club pavilion stood in Shirley Avenue on the opposite side of the driveway to the lodge. The line of the drive can be traced from an alleyway starting at the St James' Road end of Janson Road which leads to the stables and connects with Whithedwood Avenue. The lane continues between Whithedwood Avenue, Torquay Avenue and Bramston Road and originally went on through the grounds of the Methodist Church and ended in Shirley Avenue.

In 1909 Mr Day sold most of the park land, keeping only the house and a few acres around it. The Portswood property agent Walter Perkins bought the freehold and the Whithedwood Estates company which his family formed began building homes. By 1929 even the land around the house had been built up as Torquay, Whithedwood and Cedar Avenues. The house itself had become Banister Court School, a private school for boys, as 3 Whithedwood Avenue. During World War II it was a Civil Defence centre and afterwards it was used as temporary accommodation for the homeless. It was finally demolished in 1950.

The stables and coach house still remain and can be seen up an alleyway near the St James' Road end of Janson Road. The stables are now used as a warehouse by a fruit and vegetable supplier. Inside, the tethering rings and traces of the bases of stalls show that there was stabling for about ten horses. There was a small tack room next to this and a coach house with double doors. Upstairs there was living accommodation for grooms and the coachman. Sections of the high brick wall which originally surrounded the kitchen garden remain. An archway from the stable yard gives access to the now ruined garden. The weather vane on the coach house is worth noting, it depicts a running fox.

The gardens of the house were beautiful as this old photograph of the walled garden shows. Cedar Avenue takes its name from the trees on the lawn. The coach house is on the right of this view.

SHIRLEY'S PUBLIC HOUSES
Dave Goddard

In 1878 a pamphlet was published by The Temperance Society calling Southampton 'an intemperate city', and no wonder: there were no fewer than 522 licensed premises (or about one for every 150 people). Shirley had its fair share, and it is the intention of this chapter to try and recall some well known, (and not-so-well-known) pubs in Shirley. Some are long gone, others have changed their name, but most remain as they were, in name if not in features.

Firstly, the most important link in the chain, the supplier of the 'raw materials', the breweries. Several of these were dotted around the town, the single major supplier being Scrase's Star Brewery, situated behind the Star Hotel in the High Street, which supplied over 80 public houses. Then there was Cooper's Brewery, in York Buildings, supplying 74 pubs, and, of course, Strong's of Romsey (now part of the Whitbread Group) who still hold a strong presence today. (No pun intended!) Several other breweries were active in the town, and supplied the Shirley area with their wares. Shirley was well blessed (?) with many pubs, with Church Street and Cannon Street (now sadly gone) boasting no less than nine pubs between them. In Cannon Street these included the *Gardener's Arms*, the *Golden Butt*, the *Nag's Head* (during the time when the road was known as Pound Street). None of these pubs are in existence today. In Church Street the *Black Horse*, the Star and the *King's Arms* reigned supreme, but only the latter remains now.

If we travel down Shirley High Street towards Town, we start at the *Windsor Castle* and then come to the *Crown Hotel*, a Grade II listed building and the last pub still standing on that side of the road until you reach the centre of Southampton. Of course, the infamous *White Hart* also stood on this side until its licence lapsed in 1982, and now a drug store stands in its place. Crossing over the road we find the *Salisbury Arms* on the corner of Newman Street, and then the *Shirley Hotel* on the next corner. Travelling down the High Street we come to the *Rising Sun*, the *Rover Inn*, the *Stile Inn*, the *Sidford* (now renamed the *Pig and Whistle*), the *Park Hotel*,

and the *Osborne Hotel*. The *Sidford* took its name from a village of the same name that was nearby. *Uncle Tom's Cabin* in Sir George's Road disappeared before the start of the twentieth Century.

It is worth noting that after leaving the *Crown Hotel*, if you walk down the same side of the road to Commercial Road, then left into Hill Lane, and continue along this seemingly endless road, the first pub on the same side is the *Bellemoor Tavern*, an inn dating back to the 1860s, when the licensee went by the colourful name of Thankful Joy! However, back to Shirley to continue our tour.

Let's turn the corner at the *Pig and Whistle*, turn right into Park Road, and we come to the *Wellington Arms*, known as the *Swan Inn* until 1975. In the early part of this century Barlow's Brewery owned this pub, then Brickwood's, and the Whitbread Group in 1971. It is now a Free House. Along to the *Freemantle Hotel* in Paynes Road, demolished by an air raid in 1940, temporarily re-built in 1941; the present building dates from 1956. Turning north up Park Road into Firgrove Road, we find that on the corner with Dyer Road stood the *Globe Inn*, which had a beer licence before 1869 and was owned by several breweries in its life before becoming a private residence in 1957. West of Firgrove Road, in Albany Road, we see the *Freemantle Arms*, a beer house until 1957, when it received a full licence from the blitzed *Pound Tree Inn* in Pound Tree Road.

At the end of Firgrove Road we come to the *Duchess of Wellington*, actually situated in Wolseley Road, and known up to the end of the nineteenth century as the *Duke of Wellington*. West along Wolseley Road to Foundry Lane we come to the *Anchor and Hope*, formerly the *Andover Inn*, when the address was Wellington Road, the old name for Wolseley Road. An interesting fact about this pub is that it is the only one I know which has an entrance in three separate roads.

North along Foundry Lane and into Edward Road, to the *Bald Faced Stag*, a Marston's house now, but formerly owned by the Winchester Brewery.

Retracing our steps west of Foundry Lane, we can look in on the *Ampthill Hotel*, one of the last pubs to be built for Scrase's Brewery, in 1925, before being taken over by Strong's (now Whitbread). Not far from here we find the *Englishman*, on the corner of English Road and Imperial Avenue. This pub received its licence in 1904, surrendered from the *Yacht Inn*, in French Street. For many years this pub was an off-licence only, belonging to the Winchester Brewery, it now being a Marston's house.

Continuing north up Foundry Lane, we eventually find ourselves in Marlborough Road, the one-time home of the *Royal Albert*, at No 23. This pub was not granted a full licence until 1960, and closed for good in 1970: a car park now stands on the site. This circuit brings us close to our original starting point in Church Road and Shirley High Street. If we now continue north up Shirley High Street into Romsey Road, and turn left into Shirley Park Road, we find ourselves at the *Park Inn*, a pub dating back to the early 1860s, when it was known as the *Park*

Tavern, and Carlisle Road was Union Road. It has been owned by several breweries throughout its life, and is now the property of Wadworth's.

Returning to Romsey Road and continuing north we come to the *Blacksmith's Arms*, known for three years in the 1990s as *Ringside*, but changing back to its original name in 1993. The landlord in 1916 was fined 10/- (50p) for allowing 'treating' in the pub. During the First World War the Defence of the Realm Act made it illegal to buy rounds ('treating'), and introduced the strict licensing laws that ended in 1988. The purpose of this law was to ensure that workers did not spend all their time and money in the pubs. I'd sure we all know some people who THINK that the 'treating' law is still in force! Across the road we enter the *Old Thatched House*, the only thatched pub left in Southampton; the building may be several hundred years old. Before the Second World War it was owned by the People's Refreshment House Association. It was taken over by Bass Charrington in 1974.

The present site of the Scotthall garage was once a brewery in the old buildings of Shirley Mill.

If we now proceed east along Winchester Road, we come to Warren Avenue, home of the *Ice House Inn*. This pub dates from 1912, and stands next to the site of an earlier pub of the same name, which was built over an ice-pit of the 1860s, probably constructed by the Royal Mail Steam Packet Company. Further along Winchester Road is the *Malvern*, by comparison a modern pub, dating back to the early 1930s, when the licence from the *Antelope Hotel* was transferred here: previously it was a private residence.

Partly retracing our steps along Winchester Road we find the *Stratton*, in Stratton Road. This pub was opened in 1970 by Bass Charrington, and was then called the *Shield and Dagger*. The name changed to the *Stratton* in 1990, when it was taken over by Wadworth's Brewery. Also in Stratton Road were the *Globe Inn*, standing on the corner with Vaudrey Street, a Brickwood's house when it closed in

1966, and the *Lion Inn*, at the junction with Wellington Street, which was not granted a full licence until 1954, and was demolished in 1968.

Continuing to the south-west we find the *Griffin* on the corner of Victor Street and Anglesea Road, originally called the *Forester's Arms*. Welsh's Lion Brewery (whose brew house was at Apsley Villa in Anglesea Road), leased the premises in 1871, for the princely sum of £20 per annum! It is believed that the name *Griffin* came from the Griffin Brewery at Chiswick when the pub was sold to Fuller, Smith and Turner of Chiswick in 1898.

Again we are back close to our starting point, and if I've missed a pub or two on the way, my apologies! Our journey now resumes at Four Posts Hill, and we travel out of town along Millbrook Road. The *Beehive Inn* was at 10 Millbrook Road. It closed in

Local Studies Collection, Central Library

The Globe in Stratton Road.

1977, and the site is occupied by a modern office building. Next comes the *Key and Anchor*, still standing on the corner with Cracknore Road, belonging to the Whitbread Group. A little further on at 150 Millbrook Road was the *Eagle Hotel*, another Whitbread house that closed in 1981. Not a cheap place to drink, this! In 1920 the landlady was fined £50 (a tidy sum in those days) for selling 'overpriced whisky from an unmarked bottle'. The next pub was the *Maltster*, not far from an old Vincent and Elliott's oast house from which it derives its name. Its original name was the *Millbrook Railway Hotel*, later the *Railway Hotel*, and finally the *Maltster* in the 1960s. The licence was allowed to lapse on New Year's Eve 1975 and the building was demolished shortly afterwards. Mountbatten Way now runs over the site.

The *Royal Mail* was next, a coaching inn reputed to be over 300 years old, and standing on the bank of Tanners Brook. The licence was suspended in 1967 in order that Millbrook Road could be widened, and the westbound carriageway now runs over its resting place. Last, but not least, on this side was the *Oliver Cromwell*, reputed to have received its name from the fact that the man himself stayed the night at this 400 year old inn on his way through Southampton during the Civil War. This too was demolished to make way for the dual carriageway in 1967.

Returning towards town we find the *Sailor's Return* on the north side of Millbrook Road, and on the corner of Waterhouse Lane. This pub dates back to the 1860s, when it belonged to Cooper's Brewery; it being part of the Watney Group today. it was refurbished in 1983 at a cost of £50,000. In Waterloo Road we find the *Star and Garter* at the junction with Park Road, and the *Waterloo Arms*, on the site of the original pub of that name which dated back to the 1860s. It was taken over by Strong's Romsey Brewery in the 1920s, when the present building was probably erected. It was again taken over by Salisbury's independent Hop Back Brewery in 1991.

I seem unable to find a circular route for the remaining pubs, and I therefore propose to say a brief word about each of them in a random order. In Wimpson Lane we have the *Bricklayer's Arms*, a country pub from at least 1817 until the advent of the Millbrook Housing Estate, and now a busy local

City Heritage Collections

Old malt kiln, near Millbrook Station.

belonging to the Watney Group. Down the road a few hundred yards was the *Royal Oak*, about 300 years old when it was pulled down in 1965. A new pub of the same name was erected in the same year at a cost of £29,000, and has been part of the Whitbread Group since 1969.

Further south near the Millbrook roundabout is the *Swan Inn*, a pub with a varied history. The earliest record shows a licensed premises here in 1851, by the name of the *Swan Inn*, but in the 1950s when road work took place the pub found itself in a quiet cul-de-sac. However, the new by-pass soon proved inadequate for the volume of traffic, and in the late 1960s Millbrook Flyover was opened, and the *Swan* was demolished. A new pub was erected at a cost of £40,000, opened in 1968, and called the *Fighting Cocks*. The pub became the property of the Whitbread Group in 1971, and reverted to the original name in 1988.

East of here, in Regents Park Road, we find the *Regents Park Hotel*, a large Watney's house, originally built for Cooper's Brewery in the 1930s, having received the surrendered licence from the *Mariners Inn* on the Town Quay. My journey ends at the *King George Hotel*, named in honour of King George V, and granted a licence in 1933. Again, built for Cooper's Brewery, and (again!) a Watney's house.

Well, that's the end of my story, and no doubt some omissions have occurred, for which I can only apologise. I am sure that this article will provoke many arguments, but I hope that it will settle a few as well! My thanks and acknowledgements go to the many people who have 'phoned, written, and just plain stopped me in the street to offer their memories. A special tribute must be paid to my friend, Tony Gallaher, of Ringwood, without whose help this chapter could certainly not have been written. He has shared with me his manuscripts and research, painstakingly gathered over the years, saving me hours of work, and I congratulate him on the publication of his 'Southampton's Inns and Taverns'.

QUEEN VICTORIA'S JUBILEE MEMORIAL DRINKING FOUNTAIN
A G K Leonard

Queen Victoria's Jubilee in 1887 prompted great feelings of loyalty and patriotism, expressed in widespread celebrations of the occasion and pride in the achievements of the first fifty years of her reign, which had seen remarkable progress in Britain, alike in political developments towards more representative democracy and in improvements in the level and quality of life for most of her subjects.

Southampton celebrations began with a sumptuous Mayoral banquet and a civic church service, leading up to the events of Jubilee Day (June 21) and the following day, which included gun salutes, processions, sports, band concerts and other entertainments, treats for children and old folks, bonfires and fireworks.

At Shirley (not incorporated into the borough until 1895) a necessarily more modest programme was arranged by the local committee, set up at a public meeting and headed by the Vicar, the Reverend A D Burton. Residents gave generously to provide treats for children, a procession to a sports meeting, a "meat tea" for the aged poor, music and, of course, a fireworks display.

The Jubilee committee afterwards found itself with a surplus in hand and called another public meeting to consider how best to apply this balance to give Shirley a permanent Jubilee memorial. There were hopes of providing a public reading room and institute, or laying out a recreation ground, but funds were insufficient for such schemes and the committee settled for a "Jubilee Memorial Drinking Fountain". The members of the "Fountain Committee" enlisted the interest of John Haysom, principal in the old-established firm of Garret and Haysom (East Gate Masonry Works) and carried matters forward through a deputation received on January 8, 1889 at a meeting of the Shirley and Freemantle Local Board of Health, to which the proposed design was shown. The Board unanimously agreed to its erection, and referred the siting and other arrangements to a sub-committee.

Later that month, its recommendation that the fountain should be placed on the west side of Shirley High Street, opposite the "Salisbury Arms", caused a division of opinion among Board members. This site was approved only after an amendment favouring a position *on the east side of the road adjoining General Lewis' property* had been voted down 6 - 3. There was evidently some strength of local feeling on the matter, for when it met again on February 5, the Board had before it a memorial signed by forty-one Shirley residents objecting to the site selected, while one of the Board members gave notice that at its next meeting he would move that the previous resolution be rescinded. Mr Armstrong duly put this proposition on March 5, but lost the vote 7 - 2. This curious little dispute having been settled, the way was clear for the erection of the memorial fountain. On Wednesday afternoon, April 3, 1889, *in the presence of a large concourse of spectators, notwithstanding that the weather was very unpropitious, a drizzling rain falling and a cold wind blowing* (as the Southampton Times reported), it was unveiled by Major General Lewis. He handed it over to the Chairman of the Local Board, *with the full assurance that, under the management and direction of that body, the fountain will for many years to come give forth an ever-flowing stream of pure water for the benefit of the inhabitants of Shirley*. He was supported by Board members, the organising committee and assorted local dignitaries and well-wishers. They listened to several speeches of thanks and congratulations, echoing the General's sentiments that the fountain would be *an ornament to our village*, a real benefit to the community, and that its design was *very tasteful and admirably carried out*, reflecting great credit upon Mr Haysom, who designed and superintended the entire work.

His composition was a handsome construction of the hardest brown bed Portland stone and polished red granite columns, considered somewhat Gothic in its character. The lower part incorporated a large stone basin, facing the roadway, for horses and cattle, with a small trough for dogs on the ground beside it; opposite, on the pavement side, was the bowl for human use, with cups attached, served by a push valve water supply through lion's head masks. Over the fittings was placed the inscription: *Erected A.D. 1889 with the balance of the fund subscribed by the people of Shirley and district to commemorate the Jubilee of Her Majesty Queen Victoria, 1837-1887.*

Above the cap of the pedestal, four granite columns supported a decorative conical finial or light spire, topped by a Royal crown. Around a moulded cornice, raised lettering carried a quotation from Tennyson's "Ode to the Queen": *She wrought her people lasting good.* Between the columns was a fountain, intended to play on special occasions; water from it ran through a gargoyle into the horse trough, while the surplus from the drinking fountain supplied the dog trough. However elaborate the memorial structure, Victorians did not wish to waste precious water!

In 1898 Southampton Corporation bought out the private company which from 1879 had operated horse-drawn trams and (having previously acquired the electricity company with that object) lost little time in introducing its own electric tram services. The first section to be electrified in 1901 was that from the Junction to Shirley. Its terminus in Shirley High Street was then beside Park Street, but in 1911 the line was extended some 200 yards further north, to a point beside Newman Street. The Jubilee memorial fountain on the pavement by this corner, outside "The Salisbury Arms" (to which the Council fixed its Tramways Clock) then became a point of congestion for passengers boarding the trams. In 1913 this problem was several times discussed by, and between, the Council's Works and Tramways committees. In May the former agreed to the removal of the fountain to an approved site, on condition that the latter bore the cost, which it proved unwilling to do. Seeking to resolve the impasse, the Borough Engineer's report to the September meeting of the Works Committee included the rather tart statement *I shall thank your committee to decide the position in which this fountain shall be placed.* The question

FGO Stuart postcard c. 1907.

was then referred to a sub-committee, which duly visited the site and returned with the recommendation *that the Tramways Committee be asked to arrange for passengers leaving Shirley to board the cars at a point opposite No. 107 Shirley High Street, in order to remove the congestion at the fountain and to obviate the removal of the structure.* In December, the Tramways Committee instructed its manager to give effect to this suggestion.

The fountain was allowed to remain in its original position for another ten years, until being dismantled and re-erected across the road, to stand on the pavement outside the shops at the beginning of Romsey Road. There it stood until the 1970s, when it suffered impact damage from a lorry and was removed, to spend several years in a Corporation store, before being repaired and set up again in 1976 in the present shopping precinct.

ANONYMOUS GIFT

A year before the erection of its Jubilee memorial fountain Shirley had its first drinking fountain and horse trough, as the gift of an unknown benefactor. Standing for over a century at the foot of Shirley Road, by the junction of Four Posts Hill and Millbrook Road, it has been well cared for by the Corporation and now occupies a neatly paved area that separates it from passing traffic. In the days before the internal combustion engine replaced horse power it was, of course, more accessible to pedestrians and animals who could safely stop to refresh themselves there.

Today, few motorists spare it more than a glance as they drive past and it is, perhaps, best observed, albeit only briefly, from the upper deck of a bus, other traffic allowing. A granite horse trough on a pair of cylindrical supports (the legs of which may have held water for dogs) fronts a stone pillar drinking fountain topped by a ball finial. The stonework has scroll decorations, with a relief carving of a lion's head, from which water once flowed. Over the hood around it is carved the short inscription *Thou preserveth man and beast*, with the date A.D. 1888 above.

There is no indication of the occasion for its erection or its donor. She was a lady who evidently wished simply to help her fellow creatures slake their thirsts, without seeking recognition of her philanthropy. All that can now be discovered of her is an entry in the minute book of the Shirley and Freemantle Local Board of Health (preserved in the City Archives Office); under the heading *Drinking Fountain at Four Posts* it records that on March 20, 1888 Mr Miles moved that *this Board begs to express its thanks to the lady who has presented anonymously a drinking fountain to the District. The Board considers it to be of much value and feels confident that it will alleviate much discomfort during the ensuing heat of summer. They thank her for her gift which will serve a purpose of great utility and be an ornament to the district.* The motion was carried unanimously and Mr Miles *was asked to convey the thanks of the Board to the lady.*

Extracted, with permission, from the forthcoming book SOUTHAMPTON MEMORIALS OF CARE FOR MAN AND BEAST, by A G K Leonard.

HILL AND UPPER SHIRLEY DURING WORLD WAR TWO
Rosaleen Wilkinson

The history of the war years in Southampton has been explored in several interesting and well researched books, but some older Shirley residents have other personal stories which throw light on the wartime experiences of ordinary people.

In Southampton City Record Office is a remarkable hand written record of every air-raid alert in Shirley which was kept by Mrs E Goulty of 20 Whithedwood Avenue. The first alert was on 7th June 1940. She noted bombs in Regents Park Road on 19th June, and on 27th August in Pentire Avenue. As the year went on the raids became more frequent and severe, culminating in the raids of November and December which left the centre of Southampton virtually destroyed. In 1940 Mrs Goulty recorded 359 alerts, 206 in daylight and 153 at night. Shirley suffered considerable damage, in St James' Road, Malmesbury Road, Colebrook Avenue, Luccombe Place and Pentire Avenue. On 13th June 1941 there was even an incendiary bomb on the chicken yard at Edward's Nurseries in Bellemoor Road. The number of raids decreased to 227 in 1943, but flying bombs were a new hazard in 1944.

The last air raid alert was from 7.40 to 7.50 pm on Sunday 5th November 1944. The total number of alerts recorded by Mrs Goulty over the six years of war was 1,604, with 990 being daylight raids and 614 at night. Mrs Goulty concludes her diary with 'V.E. May 8th 1945' and FINIS neatly written in capitals.

Heavy raids at the end of 1940 not only destroyed much of Central Southampton, but also caused severe damage in suburban areas as well. On the night of 17th November 1940 land-mines fell on Alexandra Road in Hill. Freda Lanham, now a retired Headmistress, but then a young teacher, had a miraculous escape from a direct hit on her home.

For health reasons her mother found sleeping outside the house in a standard Anderson shelter difficult, although they shared one with a neighbour.

The Lanhams arranged to have a specially strengthened shelter made inside the house and furnished it with bunks and useful items including some solid mahogany dining chairs. On 16th November a cousin of mother's, Mrs Judd, came to Saturday tea as usual but as it was teeming with rain decided to stay the night instead of going home. Their friend, Mrs Daniels, who was afraid of sleeping alone in her own Anderson shelter, also joined them at bedtime. In the early hours of the morning the house suffered a direct hit by a land mine and Freda's parents and their friends were killed. Freda herself was miraculously saved when a beam crashed down onto one of the strong mahogany chairs, trapping her, but preventing anything else crushing her. Rescuers pulled Freda from the wreckage hours later at great danger to themselves as masonry threatened to fall down on them. After a hospital check up she was driven by ambulance to a relative's home and taken in with nothing left of her possessions except the night-dress she was wearing at the time.

Norman Walton has lived in Luccombe Road since the houses were built in 1935. During the war he was in a reserved occupation with the asphalt manufacturing company, Limmer and Trinidad, based in Chandlers Ford. The firm laid the runways at the wartime airfields of Tangmere, West Hampret, Holmesley, and Beaulieu. They re-surfaced all the roadways on the Common ready for use by the army and also supplied water-proof decking for naval and merchant shipping in the docks.

Southampton was well advanced in its preparation for war in some respects and Mr Walton took an ARP (Air Raid Precautions) warden's training course at the Audit House in 1938. Wardens were trained in First Aid, identifying gas, rescue work, fire fighting, and dealing with incendiary bombs. Norman was based at the ARP Shirley 5 post on the Common in a small brick building in the yard of the Keeper's cottage by the Bellemoor Gate. Each warden had set hours of duty at the post where the

Shirley ARP Unit no 7, 1942. The instructor, Mr Rowlands, is in the centre.

telephone had to be continuously manned ready to give advance warning of raids. If the sirens went all wardens were expected to report, in uniform, to their Post.

The worst raids in Upper Shirley were when land mines were dropped in Luccombe Road and Pentire Avenue. Mr Walton vividly recalled standing outside his shelter watching the mines floating down on parachutes brightly lit up by search lights. Moments later there was a massive explosion as a house on the corner of Pentire Avenue and Luccombe Road received a direct hit, killing a young couple and their new-born baby in the shelter. Houses all along the top of Pentire Avenue were flattened and debris was flung as far as the end of Luccombe Road. Norman got out his bike to try to reach the scene quicker but it was impossible to ride with so many bricks in the road. When Luccombe Place was hit the walls of one

house were demolished so completely that the roof was resting on the ground, but nobody was badly hurt.

In May 1942 Norman joined the Home Guard which trained at the Drill Hall in Millbrook. He was in an anti-aircraft battery. They were equipped with a crudely made contraption with two rockets on rails and were taught how to set the bearings and to fire them. He never actually fired one in anger but they would not have been very effective as they only had a maximum height of 3,000 yards. Their Home Guard Platoon was on duty one night in eight at the battery at Marchwood under the command of the Royal Artillery. For a time a lorry picked them up at the Civic Centre and then later they went by train to Marchwood and marched the rest of the way to the gun station. However, at the end of 1943 the Marchwood battery was closed down. No reason was given at the time but they later discovered that the site was used in the preparation for PLUTO (Pipe line under the Ocean) in readiness for D Day in 1944. A survey of the activities of the 71st Hants and Isle of Wight Home Guard HAA Battery was made on its closure. There had been 65 actions, 450 call-outs for action stations, 770 rounds fired and 2 'Category A' credits (or near misses). *While we have always looked forward to a target figure of, at least, one round per man and one Hun per troop, the enemy has not obliged and we have to be content with two Category A credits, both of which fall to C Troop.*

I n the years when our Country

was in mortal danger

NORMAN ALFRED CHARLES WALTON

who served 20 May 1942 to 31 December 1944

gave generously of his time and

powers to make himself ready

for her defence by force of arms

and with his life if need be.

George R.I.

THE HOME GUARD

Norman Walton

A final Christmas dinner was held for 102 battery on 17th December 1943. The back of the menu had a suitable poem printed on it.

The 'powers that be' decided
In the interest of the state
To invite a bunch of likely lads
Who'd parade one night in eight.

They rolled up in their dozens,
They rolled up by the score,
But the 'powers that be' kept yelling
We want more and more, and more.

They trained them in the factory
They trained them on the site
The blokes were working hard all day
And half the blooming night.

They turned up in the sunshine
They turned up in the rain
They went on bikes and lorries
And finally by train.

Some took it very seriously
Some took it as good fun
And hoped that 102 one night
Would 'poop off' at the Hun.

They went away to Hordle
To do a practice shoot
They peeled potatoes, did their guards
And didn't care a hoot.

Now the poor old Battery
Lies buried in the ground
Did its best and made a show
But never fired a round.

Edna and Phyllis Nicholls are also long-time residents, Bellemoor Road was still a country lane when they went to live there in 1923. When the war started Edna already held a driving licence so she became an ambulance driver for a while but soon transferred to an ARP unit up on the Common.

The sisters are great animal lovers and during the war they owned two wire haired terriers. They had no proper air-raid shelter, so during raids Edna would sit under the heavy dining room table with one dog whilst Phyllis sat in the under-stairs cupboard with the other. Edna particularly remembered the night of 30th November 1940 when there were very heavy raids on Southampton. As the sisters sat in their safe places hour after hour listening to the whistling of falling bombs and huge explosions they became aware of a scratching noise at the front door. When Edna crept out to open it she found a little terrier dog there and recognised it as one they had bred and given to an aunt in Dyer Road, Shirley. It turned out that the house in Dyer Road had been bombed but the dog had escaped and at the height of the raid had run back to its original home.

For many schoolchildren the coming of war brought evacuation to country towns and villages away from the attacks expected on Southampton. The Grammar School for Girls in Hill Lane was evacuated to Bournemouth in 1939 and some of the ex-pupils still have vivid memories of this time. Their maiden names have been used.

Evacuation Day had arrived. Early in the morning we assembled in the school hall with our names on labels around our necks and gas masks at the ready. It must have taken considerable organisation to transport an entire school and luggage, but in due course we were on the train and on our way to Bournemouth. It was quite exciting and felt like a holiday until we finally arrived in a large hall. Then it suddenly seemed strange and frightening to have left home and to be living with strangers. The next morning we heard Neville Chamberlain on the radio declare that we were at war with Germany and so we were there to stay. Later on in the war Bournemouth became the target for hit and run raids when usually a lone aeroplane would fly over, drop bombs and leave hastily. One day I was returning from school and suddenly there was a raider overhead and the spatter of bullets. I dived under a bench on the pavement and was lucky to avoid injury. Peggy Oxborough

The staff and sixth form who were over sixteen did fire watching from dusk to dawn when two staff and two girls were on duty each night. When it was not their shift the girls slept on camp beds in the staff room. If there was an air raid warning all four had to get up and be ready. We used to have practice sessions with a stirrup pump. Celia Broad

The time running up to D-Day in June 1944 stays in the memory as a period when Bournemouth and the south coast were bursting at the seams with troops of all nationalities. We were studying for School Certificate and D-Day memories to me are of working away at the examination papers with the sound of heavy aircraft overhead, many towing gliders full of paratroopers. Joan Fathers

After the war the girls returned to the Hill Lane buildings. The first Christmas we were there some German POW's were working in the grounds and at the Carol Service they filed in and stood at the back of the hall. We sang Silent Night and were suddenly aware of men's deep voices from behind us joining our girlish sopranos as we sang this German carol. It was very moving. Roma Phillips

The Common was used as a military camp throughout the war, and access for civilians was restricted during the build-up to D-Day in 1944. American and British tanks and army lorries were parked in their hundreds along the streets near the Common, in Shanklin Road, Pentire Avenue, Bellemoor Road and Melrose Road. Empty houses were commandeered by the military.

Edna and Phyllis Nicholls used to go to the Avenue Hall to help make sandwiches for the troops: they were always beetroot sandwiches. They befriended an English soldier called Reg Brown who was guarding a tank in Bellemoor Road. He used to come in for meals and made them a kennel and took the dogs for walks. He managed to send them a field card after the D-Day landings, but they never heard any more of him after that.

Preparations were made to receive casualties from the D-Day landings at the Borough (now the General) Hospital. The lower wards were cleared of civilian patients ready for the expected casualties of the invasion and experienced nursing sisters were brought from London. Grace Tweed had not liked the idea of working in a munition factory so when the war came she had decided to train for nursing. She lived in Vincent Avenue off Winchester Road so the Borough Hospital was an ideal posting for her. Discipline was quite strict for the young women living in the Nurses' Home, a pass was required if they wanted to go out in the evening. Punctuality at meal times was expected and no excuse was acceptable: every meal began and ended with prayers led by Matron or a senior Sister.

Norman Walton's Home Guard platoon had been transferred to an Ack-ack battery at Chandlers Ford, on the site of Asda. On the night of 5th June 1944 the platoon was told to report early and instead of resting in their hut until a raid warning came, they had to bed down around the guns to be instantly ready. They were to protect the planes and gliders which were going over in waves on their way to the D-Day landings, but the expected retaliatory German raids never came.

When the first D-Day casualties arrived at the Borough Hospital many young nurses were unprepared for the horrific injuries and were initially very upset. Later they got used to it and were expected to socialise with badly disfigured and burned soldiers and airmen at hospital dances put on for the benefit of military patients to cheer them up.

When the war ended Grace Tweed was on night duty. The sister rang up at midnight and told her she could put all the lights on now, the war was over, and she could give all the men a cup of tea.

Bibliography

Bunyard, B M, 1941 *The Brokage Book of Southampton 1439-40* Southampton Record Series

Connor, W J, 1978 *The Southampton Mayor's Book of 1606-8* Southampton Record Series

Coleman, O, 1960-1 *The Brokage Book of Southampton 1443-4* Southampton Record Series

Davies, Rev J S, 1883 *A History of Southampton*

Dudall J, *A Memoir of the Rev. James Crabb*

Gallaher, T, 1995 *Southampton's Inns and Taverns*

Godwin, H, 1904 *The Civil War in Hampshire*

Guly, M, *St Boniface's Church, Shirley - Parish Memoirs*

Hampshire Record Office, 1976 *Sir Henry Whithead's Letter Book 1601-14*

Hearnshaw F J C and Hearnshaw D M, 1905-8 *Southampton Court Leet Records* Southampton Record Society

Hughes, E, and White, P, 1991 *The Hampshire Hearth Tax Assessment 1665*

James, T B, 1979 *The Third Book of Remembrance of Southampton 1514-1602* Vol 4 (1590-1602) Southampton Record Series

Leonard, A G K, 1984 *Stories of Southampton Streets*

Leonard, A G K, 1989 *More Stories of Southampton Streets*

Local Studies Group *Shirley* Suburbs of Southampton Book III

Merson, A L, 1952-65, *The Third Book of Remembrance of Southampton, 1514-1602* 3 vols, Southampton Record Series

Moody, B, 1992 *Southampton's Railways*

Munby, J ed 1982 *Domesday Book, vol 4: Hampshire* Phillimore

Patterson, A Temple, 1966-1975 *A History of Southampton 1700-1914* 3 vols Southampton Record Series

Patterson, A Temple, 1970 *Southampton: a biography*

Platt, C, 1973 *Medieval Southampton: the port and trading community A D 1000 - 1600*

Platt, C, 1978 *Medieval England, a Social History and Archaeology from the Conquest to 1600 AD*

Rance, A, 1986 *Southampton, an Illustrated History*

Russel, Dr A D, 1991 *Report on the excavations at 24 - 38 Northlands Road, Southampton* Southampton City Council Heritage Section

Smith, M, 1992 *Report on archaeological investigations at the site of the former Unigate Dairy Depot at Hill Lane, Southampton* Southampton Archaeology

Stewart, B, and Cutten, M, *The Shayer Family of Painters*

Willis, A J, and Merson, A L, 1968 *A calender of Southampton Apprenticeship Registers, 1609-1740* Southampton Record Series

Welch, E, 1964 *Southampton Maps from Elizabethan times* Southampton Record Series

The authors also used a wide variety of other sources in their research, including contemporary newsapaper accounts, maps, guides and street directories, the Victoria County History, the Millbrook parish registers, and census returns.

THE AUTHORS

Rosaleen Wilkinson has lived all her life in Southampton. A graduate in Social Sciences, she developed an interest in local history when she gave up teaching in Special Education to bring up her family.

Philippa Newnham lived in Shirley for some years. Later, when following a course at Southampton Technical College, she wrote this piece for her final project.

Veronica Green is a librarian, working at Southampton Reference Library. She is also the archivist for the Southampton Methodist Circuit, and a lay preacher.

John Guilmant is a local historian, author and broadcaster. His books include six volumes of the History of Scouting in Southampton, and The Story of Shirley.

A G K Leonard: historian and freelance writer. Author of several books and numerous articles on Southampton local history and biography.

Reg Macdonald worked for the South Hants Motor Company at St Mary's and at Shirley Road.

Glen Curtis: local businessman, now retired, who is a governor and Honorary Secretary of the Barlow and Ellyett Homes.

Arne Engesvik: retired Norwegian Lecturer.

Dave Goddard was born and bred in Southampton. A retired insurance agent, keen on merchant shipping, this was his first attempt at writing.

Other contributors:
Roy Hawken
Doug Huggins

THE LOCAL HISTORY FORUM

The papers in this collection were all prepared by members of the Local History Group. The first Local History Group was formed in 1978, when eight enthusiasts met under the aegis of the Central Divisional Librarian (Mr A R Richards) to record their knowledge of Bitterne and to research and then to write its history. John Guilmant took over the leadership, and the first volume in what was to become a series, the 'Stories of the Southampton Suburbs', was published and sold through the library. Further groups were formed, and volumes were published on Portswood, Shirley, Woolston, Sholing, and Hill, Freemantle and Polygon during the next ten years. In 1989 the Southampton Local History Forum was established with a membership of forty people, with John Guilmant as the first Chairman, and John Truscott as Secretary.

ACKNOWLEDGEMENTS

The City Heritage section of Southampton City Council has published this latest collection. Hilary Kavanagh and Donald Hyslop selected the material for publication which was then edited by Hilary Kavanagh and John Guilmant with assistance from Pete Cottrell and Sheila Jemima. The illustrations were photographed by John Lawrence, and the design and layout were carried out by Diane Brindle of Graphics Services, both of Southampton City Council.

John Guilmant and the members of the Local History Group are very grateful to a number of individuals and institutions for their assistance, including Mr Philip Penfold, Mr John Truscott, the staff of Southampton City Council Archives Services, the Special Collections Librarian and staff, Southern Newspapers, the National Motor Museum and the City Heritage Services Officers for their excellent support and most willing service to all our contributors.